The Programmer's Book of Rules

George Ledin Jr.
Victor Ledin

 Lifetime Learning Publications
Belmont, California

A division of Wadsworth, Inc.

With love to
HELEN S. F. K.
and
GEORGE G. L. B.

Editing, design, production supervision: Brian K. Williams
Copyediting: Edna Ilyin Miller
Interior design: Marjorie Spiegelman, Christopher Keith
Composition: Typesetting Services of California
Production art: Christine Dorsaneo

Printed in the United States of America

1   2   3   4   5   6   7   8   9   10—83   82   81   80   79

Library of Congress Cataloging in Publication Data

Ledin, George.
    The programmer's book of rules.

    Bibliography: p.
    Includes index.
    1. Electronic digital computers—Programming.
I. Ledin, Victor, joint author. II. Title.
QA76.6.L369   001.6′42   79-13746
ISBN 0-534-97993-9

Contents

PREFACE

A few strong instincts and a few plain rules.
William Wordsworth

Programmers are the unsung heroes of the computer age. They are expected to produce programs that will run the first time, that can be changed easily at the whim of any user, and that are fast, well documented, and cost effective. In other words, they are expected to perform efficiently under constant pressures.

These pressures cannot be fully appreciated by people who do not program for a living. Professional programmers earn their pay solving problems that, even when conceptually simple, demand extreme attention to a multitude of details and that are frequently quite difficult from the programming point of view.

Everybody understands what a payroll system is supposed to do, for example, but few persons know how to design and implement such a system. Fewer yet know how to do it well. Likewise, the concept of sorting can be explained to anyone in a few minutes, but actually sorting millions of customer transactions within the brutal but real constraints of a daily deadline is clearly another matter.

While there probably is no way to avoid these pressures entirely, they can be controlled and diminished by following certain rules that help streamline the programming effort. Although various rules and suggestions have appeared in many publications, the advice has been fragmented, sometimes contradictory, often inconsistent, and rarely handy.

We decided that the time was right to make such advice uniform, consistent, and accessible by putting together a quick organizational guide and reference source for programmers and students of programming. The result is *The Programmer's Book of Rules (PBR)*, a digest of programming rules, methods, and approaches that have been proposed and tested by professional programmers and computer scientists.

Inside you will find over 250 rules. These rules appear in the form of simple dos and don'ts on the left-hand pages, accompanied by supporting explanations and examples on the corresponding right-hand pages. They range from the general to the specific, and while some may seem artificial and others may seem obvious, their combined effect is to help you with your daily work and in your programming career.

The more important rules are keyed to the latest published research, with references listed at the end of each chapter. A broader selection of useful sources is given in the bibliography at the end of the book. A thorough index enables you to cross-reference some of the rules, and also supplies the connections among subjects and rules, since a particular subject important to several stages of the programming effort may be covered by several rules.

Although the classification of the rules could have been made in different ways, we decided that the three parts—"Do It for Your Client," "Do It with Style," and "Do It with Substance"—provided the most realistic orientation. An analysis of customer needs ought to be the first step in any programming endeavor. Only when you know for whom is the work intended will you know how to deal with the appearance and contents of your programming product.

We hope that this summary of the extensive and scattered literature on the practice of programming will be beneficial to all programmers. We plan to keep up with the state of the art by periodically revising and updating this book, and we welcome your corrections and recommendations.

George Ledin Jr.
Victor Ledin

Acknowledgments

George Ledin Jr. thanks his colleagues Steven A. Chapman, James N. Haag, John C. Hoff, Michael A. Kelly, Michael D. Kudlick, Richard G. Peddicord, and Ytha Y. Yu, for their counsel and unfettered exchange of views over the past decade. He is grateful to the International Federation for Information Processing (IFIP) Working Group 2.3 on Programming Methodology for the privilege of having attended and participated in one of their stimulating meetings (Zürich, Switzerland, 1974), and especially grateful to several individual members of the WG2.3 who have since become his friends, for their revolutionary common sense.

Victor Ledin appreciates the sage advice and inspiration he received from Richard J. Fateman, Susan L. Graham, Lawrence A. Rowe, and Anthony I. Wasserman. He also thanks Joseph Faletti and James Joyce for their useful comments on preliminary drafts of the manuscript.

Both authors immensely praise Theresa R. Harned, who, enduring the tedium and upheaval of multiple rewritings, cheerfully helped with the typing and the retyping.

Do It for Your Client

1

KNOW YOUR CLIENTS' NEEDS

Such things are easier said than done, I see.

Plautus, Asinaria

Fit your program to your user's needs

(See references 1, 2, 3, 4.)

Design your program so that it can be used with a minimum of tutoring

Don't expect the user to rely solely on the software manuals.

Write as few directions to the user as possible. This rule is especially important for interactive programs. An interactive program with lengthy instructions forces the user to read and study the program and to remember all its quirks before using it. Use selective prompts, if possible: Let the user choose from among instructions containing increasing levels of detail.

Make your program straightforward and general. If you cannot explain how to use your program simply and clearly, then you probably should rewrite it!

Many software manuals are often inaccurate, out of date, and hard to find. That is because changes in the software are likely to occur more rapidly and more frequently than changes in the software's documentation. The user should be able to handle your program without extensive tutoring. The daily use of your program should not be a research project. Don't expect that manuals and other reference materials will be readily available to the user.

Don't expect the user to understand the program or know the language.

Never assume that a numeric input field always will be numeric.

Place as few protocol constraints as possible on the user

Don't force the user to go through the job control language (JCL) maze.

Users want your program because it is a tool that can process their data. Users need to know

> **1** how to make their data suitable as input for your program, and
> **2** what kind of output will be produced.

Users need not know the ins and outs of your solution to their problems or the clever features of the language you used. (Of course, this information may be made available to users who may have to change or maintain your program.)

Your program should check all input before processing the data. It should use "defensive programming": that is, it should edit all input data. Even if some of the input is improper, the program still should be able to process other (proper) data correctly. The operating system or system programmer should not be forced to terminate execution of your program because of bad data.

Unlike you, users need not get involved in protocol instructions such as the job control language statements. Protocol serves to define how the program should be executed, but must not be a burden on the user. If you can, you should arrange the program's protocol so that it does not have to be changed each time the user tries a different application.

Aim your program at the widest circle of users

(See references 5, 6.)

Write as general a program as possible

Avoid writing programs that serve only single needs or solve single problems.

Do not write programs that depend on very limited kinds of input.

Explain to the user how to run the program

(See reference 7.)

Whenever possible, write programs that solve more than one problem or do more than one task. For each task, be flexible when dealing with input and output. It should be possible to use the program to do just one of the available tasks. Make sure, however, that the problems and tasks are interrelated (for example, a program used to access a data base need not also calculate mathematical functions).

Obviously, no program can solve *all* problems. However, a specific problem usually belongs to a larger class of problems. Write the program to solve the problem for the larger class, not the smaller subset.

Don't limit your explanations to *how* to use the program: explain also *when*, *where*, and *why* the program should be used.

Survey the problems that can be solved by the program

Describe in detail the data to be used in the program

Don't limit yourself to standard usage.

State what exceptions exist, how the program is expected to react to wrong or incomplete data, and how the user should interpret the error messages (diagnostics).

Show users how to apply the program to their needs. Support your explanations with actual examples of typical, complete runs. For example, if your program does time-series forecasting and if bank economists are the potential users, show a run depicting short- and long-term predictions of prime interest rate variation with shifts in money supply, and so on.

The allowable input data should be described, along with all exceptions. The program should react equally well to equivalent inputs such as 1980 and 80. For another example, 666-6530 should be just as acceptable a telephone number as 6666530 or 666 6530. And your program should not "choke" on bad data: instead, it should ask the user to supply acceptable data.

By generalizing your program, you allow it to handle unusual data. Be sure the user is aware of the exceptions and special cases. State them explicitly so that the user won't waste valuable time discovering them. Think of the program as a recipe with the usual warnings ("don't oversalt!") and the suggested substitutions ("butter *or* margarine").

Make it easy for the user to run the program

(See references 8, 9.)

Design the data entry segment of the program to handle the user's data easily

Don't straight-jacket the user with unreasonably inflexible input requirements.

Use uniform and general input formats.

Allow format-free data input, if possible.

Let the user define the program's data entry formats.

Make it easy for users to proofread their input.

Be flexible in what you allow as data. If the data is numeric, be sure that your program can handle the smallest and largest applicable numbers as input. Extended precision should be available automatically when needed. For character (or string) data, allow for the longest applicable string (for example, at least the width of a CRT screen line). If data entered by the user is incorrect or out of range, the operating system should not simply trigger a message such as "FAULTY DATA" or "DATA ERROR." Your program should explain to the user *why and how* the data is faulty.

Although your program should check the input, it also should offer the user the choice of displaying all, some, or none of the input. Don't *force* the user to inspect the input: allow him or her to make a choice. If there is a great deal of data, displaying all of it would be costly. Perhaps the user already has checked the data and need not do so again.

> # Allow the user to run the program with more than one set of data

REFERENCES

1. K. W. Morton, "What the Software Engineer Can Do for the Computer User," in *Software Engineering—An Advanced Course,* edited by F. L. Bauer, Springer-Verlag, Berlin, 1973, pages 4−11.

2. E. Hunt, G. Diehr, and D. Garnatz, "Who Are the Users? An Analysis of Computer Use in a University Computer Center," in *Proceedings of the AFIPS Spring Joint Computer Conference,* vol. 38, 1971, pages 231−238.

3. James Joyce, "Human Factors in Software Engineering," in *Proceedings of the First Computer Faire,* San Francisco, 1977, pages 56−63.

4. H. Hunke, "Some Human Engineering Aspects of Programming," in *Structured Programming,* Infotech State of the Art Report, Infotech International Ltd., Maidenhead, Berkshire, U.K., 1976, pages 265−278.

> Give the user the choice of running the program with only one set of data or with multiple data sets. Don't force the user to run your program again for each additional set of data.

5. Theodore D. Sterling, "Guidelines for Computerized Information Systems: A Report from Stanley House," *Communications of the ACM,* vol. 17, no. 11, November 1974, pages 609–613.

6. Theodore D. Sterling, "Humanizing Computerized Information Systems," *Science,* vol. 190, December 19, 1975, pages 1168–1172.

7. Donald Ervin Knuth, "Computer Programming as an Art," *Communications of the ACM,* vol. 17, no. 12, December 1974, pages 667–673.

8. Andrei P. Ershov, "Aesthetics and the Human Factor in Programming," *Communications of the ACM,* vol. 15, no. 7, July 1972, pages 501–505 (and Corrigendum, page 913.)

9. Henry M. Parson, "The Scope of Human Factors in Computer-Based Data Processing Systems," *Human Factors,* vol. 12, no. 2, March–April 1970, pages 165–175.

Do It with Style

2

SOLVE THE PROBLEM

Solving problems is a practical art, like swimming, or skiing, or playing the piano: you can learn it only by imitation and practice.

George Polya, Mathematical Discovery

Define the problem

(See references 1, 2.)

Understand it well, or have it explained to you.

Break the problem down into subproblems

(See reference 3.)

Simplify your task by analyzing the parts of the problem individually.

Each problem has three main parts: input, processing, and output. To understand a given problem, you must understand what is its *data* (input), what *operations* and *changes* are to be made to the data (processing), and what *results* and *answers* are needed (output).

By determining the three main parts of a given problem (input, processing, and output), you segment the problem into three subproblems. Determine all of the following:

Input
1 What is the form of the data?
2 How much data is there?
3 What variables are needed?
4 What formulas are needed?
5 Should only the given data be accepted?

Processing
6 What is the order of the operations on the data?
7 In what order should these results be obtained?
8 Is the processing to be done more than once?

Output
9 What results are needed?
10 What should be the results' form?

The above steps are the elements of Hierarchy plus Input, Processing, and Output (HIPO) analysis.

Practice iterative functional decomposition.

Find out what is given and what is expected

Plan your program's data entry (input) and data display (output).

Research the problem

Consult your software library

Don't duplicate someone else's work if you already have a suitable program or can buy one.

Repeatedly break the whole into logical pieces segregated by their function.

Ask yourself the following:

1 How is the data to be entered?
2 In what form will the results and answers be displayed?
3 Is anything missing?
4 Can your descriptions of data entry and data display handle exceptions?

After determining what each problem and subproblem should do, check to see if there are programs already available on your system that solve a subproblem or even the whole problem. Ask yourself the following:

1 Have you done a problem like this one before?
2 Could you use your old programs?
3 How much effort would it be to modify the old programs to fit them to the problem? Will this effort be cost-effective?

Consult the computing literature

(See reference 4.)

Don't "rediscover the wheel" if a published algorithm can be applied to the problem.

A common misconception is that it takes more time to locate a program or algorithm than it takes to write your own. Ask yourself:

1 Has the problem been solved before by someone else?
2 Has a related problem been solved before by someone else?
3 Can you use its method of solution?
4 Can you change its method of solution to fit your problem?
5 Can you redefine the problem to adapt it to a known method of solution?

You should look through books dealing with the problem area. Journal articles may contain tested programs that might be helpful. Good sources are:

1 *Collected Algorithms of the CACM.*
2 *Computing Reviews* [published monthly by the Association for Computing Machinery (ACM)].
3 *Computer Abstracts* (the British equivalent of *Computing Reviews*).
4 The numerous program and software indexes available.
5 Various software companies' bulletins or newsletters.

If a program is already available, why waste valuable human energy and time reinventing it? Know your library. Become familiar with information sources in your field. Libraries are organized information centers available to you—you should learn how to use them! The initial effort of getting to know your sources will pay off handsomely later in time and labor saved.

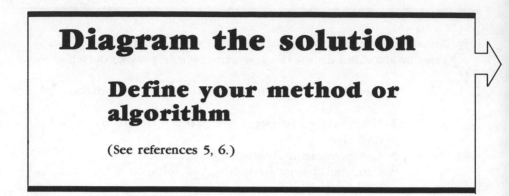

Diagram the solution

Define your method or algorithm

(See references 5, 6.)

List the method's steps

Organize your solution schematically

(See reference 7.)

Choose a recipe. Determine how the recipe suits your needs by asking yourself:

1 Does the algorithm or method solve the problem?
2 Does it give me more than I want?
3 Is anything missing?
4 Is it easy to implement?
5 Is it easy to understand?

Determine whether the steps:

1 solve the problem,
2 are in the desired order, and
3 can be altered easily to suit your needs.

Organize the:

1 data for ease of input;
2 process data so that calculations, decisions, and repetitions are done in the necessary order;
3 results so that they are easy to evaluate, read, and understand.

A schematic representation of your solution is very much like a cook book. Write it in *pseudocode* (terse English that resembles your programming language). Use decision tables (break down the solution into conditions and actions), if necessary.

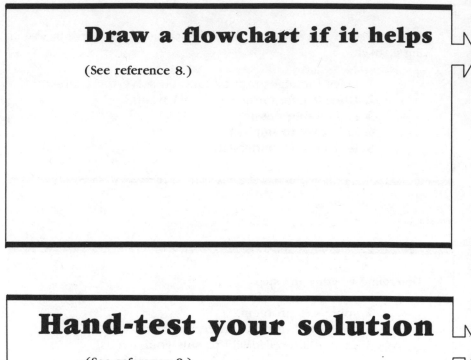

Draw a flowchart if it helps

(See reference 8.)

Hand-test your solution

(See reference 9.)

Play "computer"

Manually trace your algorithm as if it were run on the computer.

(See reference 10.)

List all transactions that occur as you go through the steps of the algorithm

A "back of the envelope" flowchart may be better than none. A good flowchart not only will help diagram the solution, but later will also provide valuable documentation.

Use a flowchart template. Stick to standard flowchart symbols. (In particular, learn your company's in-house standards.) Subdivide any large flowchart into a macrochart and several microcharts (one for each process in the macrochart). Stripe macrochart symbols to make them easily distinguishable from all others.

If you are using a structured language such as ALGOL, PASCAL, or PL/1, use structured flowcharts

Simulate the actual execution of a program before running it. Check each statement carefully to make sure that it does what you expect it to do. Make sure the data is being entered correctly and that the order of execution is correct.

For extremely complicated programs, use a *profiler* (software that provides information about the program without compiling it) to check such items as loop delimiters and nesting, procedure or sub-program calls, and variables' histories.

Conduct a problem *walkthrough* to verify that the problem has been defined correctly and that the solution meets your client's objectives. If a manual walkthrough is too tedious or too difficult, insert output statements to trace the program's action. This may be helpful at a later stage when debugging.

Keep track of all changes in the values held by the variables.

Check all the expected output.

Check boundary conditions and null input (initially empty) files.

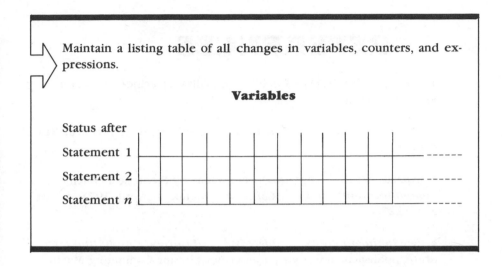

Maintain a listing table of all changes in variables, counters, and expressions.

Variables

Status after

Statement 1

Statement 2

Statement *n*

Make sure that the output (results) are what you expect. The table will help here also. Indicate clearly in the table what outputs occur and where. Is the output occurring at the correct places in your program?

Determine the following:

1 Have each record and file been described fully?
2 Is the expected volume of data to be entered into a particular file known?
3 Have the methods of file storage and maintenance been evaluated?

REFERENCES

1. George Polya, *How to Solve It* (2nd edition), Princeton University Press, Princeton, N. J., 1973.

2. Wayne A. Wickelgren, *How to Solve Problems*, W. H. Freeman, San Francisco, 1974.

3. Niklaus Wirth, "Program Development by Stepwise Refinement," *Communications of the ACM,* vol. 14, no. 4, April 1971, pages 221–227.

4. See *Bibliography and Subject Index of Current Computing Literature*, published annually by the Association for Computing Machinery. This is an index of ACM's monthly publication *Computing Reviews*, which reviews and abstracts most of the important computer science literature.

5. Doris M. Wheatley and Alan W. Unwin, *The Algorithm Writer's Guide*, Longman, London, 1972.

6. Donald Ervin Knuth, "Algorithms," *Scientific American,* vol. 236, no. 4, April 1977, pages 63–80.

7. Herman McDaniel (editor), *Applications of Decision Tables—A Reader*, Brandon/Systems Press, Princeton, N. J., 1970.

8. Ned Chapin, "Flowcharting with the ANSI Standard: A Tutorial," *Computing Surveys,* vol. 2, no. 2, June 1970, pages 119–146. (See also bibliography for books on flowcharting.)

9. Edward Yourdon, *Structured Walkthroughs* (2nd edition), Yourdon Press, New York, 1978.

10. Larry Weissman, "Psychological Complexity of Computer Programs: An Experimental Methodology," *SIGPLAN Notices,* vol. 9, no. 6, June 1974, pages 25–36.

3

KNOW YOUR PROGRAMMING LANGUAGE

In language clearness is everything.

Confucius, Analects

Choose the right language for the job   38

Select appropriate constructs   44

Choose the right language for the job

(See references 1, 2, 3, 4, 5.)

Determine the kind, quantity, and intricacy of the processing required by the problem

Determine how much output will be generated

For scientific and numerically sophisticated problems, choose FORTRAN, PL/1, APL, BASIC, ALGOL, PASCAL

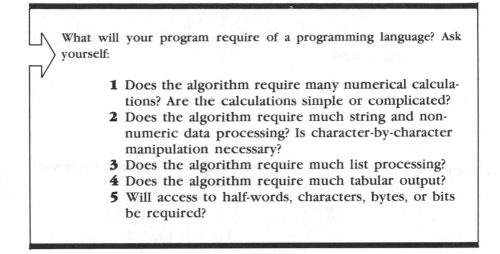

What will your program require of a programming language? Ask yourself:

> 1 Does the algorithm require many numerical calculations? Are the calculations simple or complicated?
> 2 Does the algorithm require much string and non-numeric data processing? Is character-by-character manipulation necessary?
> 3 Does the algorithm require much list processing?
> 4 Does the algorithm require much tabular output?
> 5 Will access to half-words, characters, bytes, or bits be required?

Ask yourself:

> 1 Are multiple reports to be printed?
> 2 Will file-handling facilities make the job easier?
> 3 Should the output be generated more than once?
> 4 Are predesigned forms to be used?

ALGOL, APL, FORTRAN and PASCAL are weaker in string processing than are BASIC or PL/1. Complicated formulas, especially those of the vectorial type, are represented more simply in APL. Both APL and BASIC usually are interactive, whereas the others are typically batch oriented.

For business problems, choose COBOL, BASIC, PL/1, RPG.

(See reference 6.)

For verbal or humanities problems, choose text editors, SNOBOL, FORTRAN, PASCAL, PL/1.

(See references 7, 8.)

Identify the data structures necessary for the solution of the problem

(See references 9, 10.)

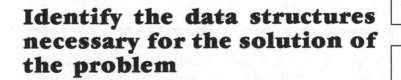

Each language has its own advantages. Some BASICs have good file-handling facilities and simplified matrix and array capabilities. COBOL is portable and is better at file handling than most other languages. RPG is simple and can be used on smaller machines. PL/1 is an "omnibus" language because it combines features of many languages. Investigate also commercially available proprietary languages such as MARK IV.

You can handle bibliographies, glossaries, thesauri, and the production and analysis of large amounts of verbal data, most easily with languages that have features powerful enough to handle text processing.

Consider lists, trees, arrays, and recursive structures.

Choose a language that has such data structures.

(See references 11, 12, 13.)

Acquaint yourself with the language's features

Choose the language that has the most directly applicable features.

BASIC has convenient (but trivial) array manipulation facilities (the MAT statements). APL has powerful array (vector) handling features. Recursion is possible with the ALGOLs, PASCAL, and PL/1, as well as in LISP and SNOBOL. Some languages, such as PASCAL, allow you to define your own data structures. Pick from among the languages available to you the one that best handles the data structures you need.

Start by comparing a new language's features with the equivalent features of a language that you know well. Try translating into this new language one of your previously written, tested, and proven programs.

Find out if the language is *extensible* (that is, if it permits its feature definitions to be extended to fit your and your client's needs.) (See reference 16.)

Remember that you may need to create interfaces.

(See reference 14.)

Know the language's data display (plotter and graphics) capabilities.

(See reference 15.)

Select appropriate constructs

Use the language's best features to advantage

(See reference 17.)

Favor constructs that require the simpler features.

Often you will need to interface your program with routines to a peripheral device, such as a plotter or a graphics terminal. You also may need to interface programs written in different languages, programs written in a high-level language with those written in assembly language, or with a program product or software package. Will the language you have chosen make this type of interface as simple as possible? Ask your computer center staff what interface capabilities are available to you. Elaborate and time-consuming interfaces are rarely worth the development effort.

Can your chosen language be used to drive plotters or graphics terminals? These devices may be "driven" by special communications routines.

Recursion is the strong point of the ALGOLs, APL, and LISP. String processing is the best feature of SNOBOL. Large data-base manipulation and self documentation are the advantages of COBOL. Languages such as GPSS, SIMSCRIPT, and SIMULA make simulation much easier.

REFERENCES

1. D. W. Barron, *An Introduction to the Study of Programming Languages,* Cambridge University Press, Cambridge, U.K., 1977.

2. Bryan Higman, *A Comparative Study of Programming Languages* (2nd edition), Macdonald/American Elsevier, London, 1977.

3. Elliott I. Organick, Alexandra I. Forsythe, and Robert P. Plummer, *Programming Language Structures,* Academic Press, New York, 1978.

4. Terrence W. Pratt, *Programming Languages: Design and Implementation,* Prentice-Hall, Englewood Cliffs, N.J., 1975.

5. Jean E. Sammet, *Programming Languages: History and Fundamentals,* Prentice-Hall, Englewood Cliffs, N.J., 1969.

6. See Bibliography, Programming Languages, pages 233–236.

7. Robert J. Dilligan, "Introductory FORTRAN Textbooks: An Overview for Humanists," *Computers and the Humanities,* vol. 7, no. 6, September–November 1973, pages 399–406.

8. James Joyce, "Extensions to PL/1 for Natural-Language Processing," *Computers and the Humanities,* vol. 6, no. 5, May 1972, pages 271–275.

9. C. A. R. Hoare, "Notes on Data Structuring," in *Structured Programming* by O.-J. Dahl, E. W. Dijkstra, and C. A. R. Hoare, Academic Press, New York, 1972, pages 83–174.

10. G. H. Mealy, "Another Look at Data," in *Proceedings of the AFIPS Fall Joint Computer Conference,* Vol. 31, 1967, pages 525–534.

11. Malcom C. Harrison, *Data-Structures and Programming,* Scott, Foresman & Company, Glenview, Ill., 1973.

12. Ellis Horowitz and Sartaj Sahni, *Fundamentals of Data Structures,* Computer Science Press, Potomac, Md., 1976.

13. Niklaus Wirth, *Algorithms + Data Structures = Programs,* Prentice-Hall, Englewood Cliffs, N.J., 1976.

14. J. C. Cluley, *Computer Interfacing and On-Line Operation,* Crane, Russak & Co., New York, 1975.

15. Thomas C. Smith and Y. C. Pao, *Introduction to Digital Computer Plotting,* Gordon & Breach, Science Publishers, New York, 1973.

16. David L. Parnas, "Designing Software for Ease of Extension and Contraction," *IEEE Transactions on Software Engineering,* vol. SE-5, no. 2, March 1979, pages 128 – 138.

17. Gerhard Goos, "Language Characteristics," in *Software Engineering—An Advanced Course,* edited by F. L. Bauer, Springer-Verlag, Berlin, 1973, pages 47 – 69.

4

MAKE YOUR PROGRAM LAYOUT READABLE

It is always the unreadable that occurs.

Oscar Wilde, The Decay of Lying

Organize your program into segments

(See reference 1.)

Provide each segment with a heading

Subdivide your program

(See references 2, 3.)

Subdivide by at least three tasks: data entry, processing, data display.

(See reference 4.)

Keep related statements together.

Be sure to indicate what each segment does. Provide headings so that at a glance you can determine the purpose of each program segment without having to hand-trace it.

Subdivide further if doing so improves clarity. For instance, indicate the input segment by origin or device group [for example, fed directly from a laboratory instrument or obtained from the tape drive (number X)]. Indicate the output segment by destination or target device (for example, card punch, tape drive, paper printer).

Statements can be related in several ways: by programming task (for example, all output statements may be clustered at the end of the program, all data entry statements at the beginning); by their role in the language (for example, all format instructions may be clumped together); or by their problem-solving purpose (for example, all format and output statements used for a particular calculation).

Insert blank lines or blank comments between segments.

Plan your program's appearance

(See references 5, 6.)

Choose a uniform width

Don't exceed a chosen maximum line width.

Break long lines into shorter ones.

Avoid putting more than one statement on a line.

Align statements of the same weight

(See reference 7.)

Indent all statements inside a particular control structure.

Indent all code within loops.

Blank lines make it easy for the eye to locate the different program segments.

Don't write ultralong statements or extrashort ones. Pick a maximum width and stick to it. Follow the approach used in typesetting books, and your program will be much easier to read.

Indent all loops and all loops within loops; indent all subprograms and all subprograms within subprograms. Your program layout should have a box-within-box appearance:

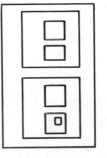

REFERENCES

1. James R. Donaldson, "Structured Programming," *Datamation,* vol. 19, no. 12, December 1973, pages 52 – 54.

2. Edward F. Miller Jr. and George E. Lindamood, "Structured Programming: Top-Down Approach," *Datamation,* vol. 19, no. 12, December 1973, pages 55 – 57.

3. Niklaus Wirth, "On the Composition of Well-Structured Programs," *Computing Surveys,* vol. 6, no. 4, December 1974, pages 247 – 259.

4. Niklaus Wirth, *Systematic Programming,* Prentice-Hall, Englewood Cliffs, N.J., 1973.

5. Daniel D. McCracken and Gerald M. Weinberg, "How to Write a Readable FORTRAN Program," *Datamation,* vol. 18, no. 10, October 1972, pages 73 – 77.

6. Dennie van Tassel, *Program Style, Design, Efficiency, Debugging, and Testing* (2nd edition), Prentice-Hall, Englewood Cliffs, N.J., 1978. See Chapter 1 ("Program Style"), pages 1 – 40.

7. Paul W. Purdom, *Program Indentation,* Indiana University, Computer Science Dept., Bloomington, Ind., Technical Report No. 54, December 1976.

5

MAKE YOUR OUTPUT MEANINGFUL AND USEFUL

Reading is not a duty, and has consequently no business to be made disagreeable.

Augustine Birrell,
Obiter Dicta: Second Series:
The Office of Literature

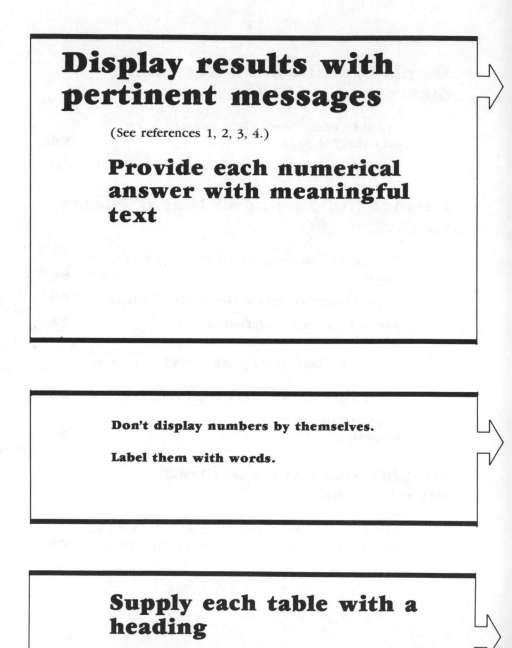

Display results with pertinent messages

(See references 1, 2, 3, 4.)

Provide each numerical answer with meaningful text

Don't display numbers by themselves.

Label them with words.

Supply each table with a heading

Print the heading on each page in which the table appears.

The following program segment

```
100 LET R = 25
110 LET S = SQR (R)
120 PRINT S
```

yields the result 5 when the program is run. The result is understandable only if you know that the 5 that was printed pertains to the calculation of the square root of 25. A clearer output would be generated by the following statement

```
120 PRINT "THE SQUARE ROOT OF"; R; "IS "; S
```

which would print not only the 5 but also the message

```
THE SQUARE ROOT OF 25 IS 5
```

Always label all your output. What makes sense to you now will be obscure later when you look at the program. Your output always should be independent of your program. It should be documented so that the user does not have to refer to the actual program for guidance. Nothing is "perfectly clear" unless you make it so!

When you are displaying a lot of related output in the form of a table, it is often redundant to attach a message to each individual entry in the table. A good practice is to provide a table heading. For example:

```
      WRITE (6,600)
600   FORMAT (1H1,"TABLE OF PRIME NUMBERS")
```

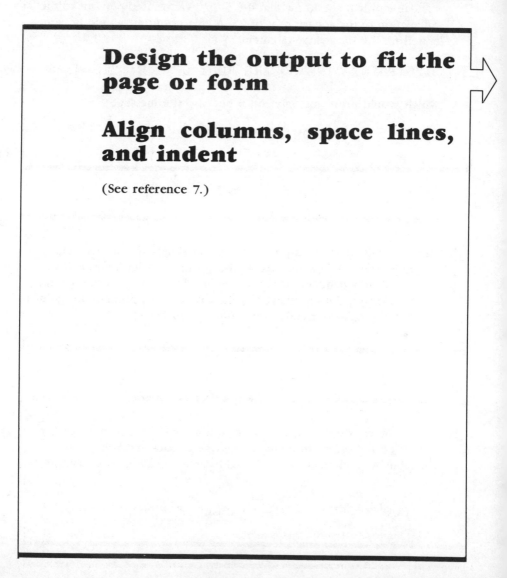

Format the output so that it is easy to read

(See references 5, 6.)

Design the output to fit the page or form

Align columns, space lines, and indent

(See reference 7.)

Design the output so that it reads easily. Even when headings and remarks appear as part of the output, you should plan the output carefully so that it is visually attractive. Involve your program's user!

Often it is not enough just to provide headings for your output. You also must align and space the output so that it matches the appropriate headings. Compare the following two outputs:

Output no. 1

```
TABLE OF SQUARES AND CUBES
OF THE FIRST FIVE NUMBERS

        1    1    1
        2    4    8
        3    9    27
        4    16   64
        5    25   125
```

Output no. 2

```
TABLE OF SQUARES AND CUBES
OF THE FIRST FIVE NUMBERS

   NUMBER   SQUARE   CUBE
      1        1       1
      2        4       8
      3        9       27
      4        16      64
      5        25      125
```

Obviously, output number two is *easier to read* and even *looks nicer*. Plan the layout of your program's output with the aid of squared paper or output layout forms.

Right-justify all numerical output.

Make sure that the decimal points are aligned.

Left-justify all non-numerical output.

Avoid lazy and fast formatting

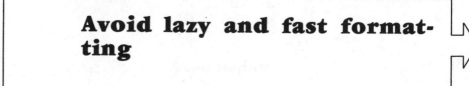

These guidelines produce clean, easy-to-read output. Examples:

ACCOUNT NO.	NAME	TOTAL IN ACCOUNT
552-74	JOHN BEEZWAX	$ 11111.11
549-80	MARY HONEY	$ 25.07
6001-66	PER TREE	$ 450.00
345-125	STAN DART	$ 0.05

"Quick and dirty" formatting of output is only a temporary solution to planning your output. *For the user, output is the most important part of the program.* In your output, you are displaying the results—the reason for the very existence of the program.

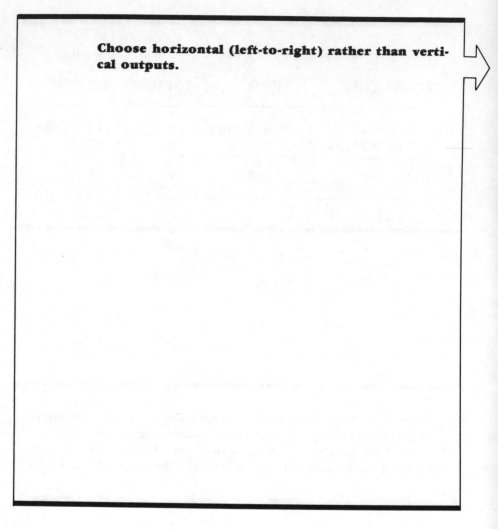

Choose horizontal (left-to-right) rather than vertical outputs.

Vertical outputs are harder to read and often do not fit entirely on a given page. Horizontal output is more "space-conscious."

Vertical output

TABLE OF FIRST 25 PRIMES

$$2$$
$$3$$
$$5$$
$$7$$
$$11$$

Oops, ran out of space ...

Horizontal output

TABLE OF FIRST 25 PRIMES

2	3	5	7	11
13	17	19	23	29
31	37	41	43	47
53	59	61	67	71
73	79	83	89	97

Got them all!

Choose useful output text

(See reference 8.)

Make sure the answers are complete

Don't ignore results that the user may have overlooked.

Provide users with all the information needed

Displaying all the changes in values of all the variables and all the intermediate values of all the counters is purposeless and wasteful. These intermediate values may be useful when you are looking for an elusive program error, but after the program has been debugged, it should display only the data entered and the results. Both the original data and the results should be clearly marked and documented.

Output should be documented so that missing output becomes obvious. Erroneous input should be labeled as such. A program that interacts with the user should ask for as much information as possible before doing any calculations or making any decisions.

Don't bury the results in unnecessary explanations and comments. Be succinct. A few sentences explaining what the results pertain to and what they mean is all you need.

Avoid obscure abbreviations, mnemonics, acronyms, or unusual symbols.

Display the user's original input

(See reference 9.)

Allow the user to proofread and edit the input before proceeding with the output

(See reference 10.)

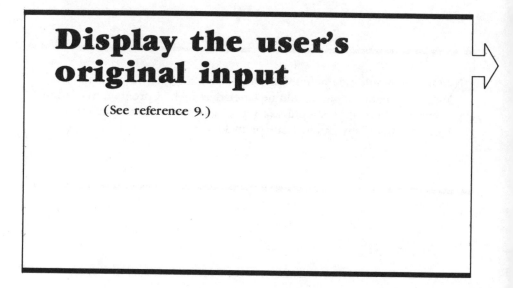

Acronyms and abbreviations in your program text are useful. However, the output should make the results clear to the user. Suppose you used SSN as a variable name in the program: in the output, you should say *Social Security Number.*

Without the original input, the user may not be able to see whether or not the results are correct and correspond to the appropriate input. If the results are not what the user expects, then the display of the original data will help in checking for possible errors. Displaying the original data becomes even more important when the user has no control over the input. A typical example is input generated by measurements coming from a laboratory instrument interfaced with the computer. The computer manipulates these numbers internally and your program uses them in its calculations. Unless these "hidden" input numbers are displayed as the program is executed, the user will not be able to determine whether the results of the calculations are correct. However, it may be desirable to pre-edit the input list (see rules below).

With an output of the original data, the user is able to check the data for possible omissions, duplications, or errors. Although your program should be able to handle erroneous data, wasted runs can be avoided if these errors are caught before the run. This preventive checking is all the more important when your program is long and costly to run.

REFERENCES

1. Franz Selig, "Documentation Standards," in *Software Engineering —Concepts and Techniques,* edited by J. N. Buxton, Peter Naur, and Brian Randell, Petrocelli/Charter, New York, 1976, pages 129–131.

2. W. M. Turski, *Computer Programming Methodology,* Heyden & Son Ltd., London, 1978. See Section 4.2.3. ("Principles of Documentation"), pages 172–179.

3. Joel D. Aron, *The Program Development Process—The Individual Programmer* (Part 1), Addison-Wesley Publishing Co., Reading, Mass., 1974. See Section 6.2 ("Documentation"), pages 186–195.

4. Robert C. Tausworthe, *Standardized Development of Computer Software,* Prentice-Hall, Englewood Cliffs, N.J., 1977. See Section 2.7 ("The Concurrent Documentation Principle"), pages 32–39.

5. G. Michael Schneider, Steven W. Weingart, and David M. Perlman, *An Introduction to Programming and Problem Solving with PASCAL,* John Wiley & Sons, New York, 1978. See Style Clinic 4-3 ("Output with Style"), pages 102–103.

6. K. V. Roberts, "Program Readability," in *Software Engineering* (Infotech State of the Art Report), Infotech International Ltd., Maidenhead, Berkshire, U.K., 1972, pages 495–516.

7. Marilyn Bohl, *A Guide for Programmers,* Prentice-Hall, Englewood Cliffs, N.J., 1978, pages 35–41.

8. Henry F. Ledgard, *Programming Proverbs,* Hayden Book Co., Rochelle Park, N.J., 1975, pages 42, 48.

9. Dennie Van Tassel, *Program Style, Design, Efficiency, Debugging, and Testing* (2nd edition), Prentice-Hall, Englewood Cliffs, N.J., 1978, pages 196–197.

10. Brian W. Kernighan and P. J. Plauger, *The Elements of Programming Style* (2nd edition), McGraw-Hill Book Company, New York, 1978. See Chapter 5 ("Input and Output"), pages 83–100.

Do It with Substance

6

PROCEED STEP BY STEP

Let all things be done decently and in order.

New Testament: I Corinthians

Write your program to read in the order in which it will execute

(See references 1, 2, 3, 4, 5, 6, 7.)

Have your program execute one instruction after another, from top to bottom

Bad

```
    IF B THEN GOTO 5
    GOTO 10
  5 X = Y
    Y = Z
 10 WRITE . . . .
```

We are branching twice needlessly in the above example when we can achieve the same results in two consecutive instructions.

Good

```
    IF NOT B THEN GOTO 10
    X = Y
    Y = Z
 10 WRITE . . . .
```

or

```
    IF B THEN
        BEGIN
            X := Y;
            Y := Z
        END
```

Avoid forward and backward references.

Make consecutive order the fundamental control structure

Arrange your program in systematic units

Use a modular structure

(See references 8, 9, 10.)

Don't "spaghettize." Eliminate as many unconditional transfers of control as possible. Avoid GOTOs.

The shortest route between two points in a program is straight and direct. Clever or circuitous routes must be avoided.

Break programs into groups of statements that can be tested and debugged apart from the rest of the program. In ALGOL, PASCAL, and PL/1, they are called blocks and procedures; in FORTRAN, functions or subroutines; in APL, main routines or functions; and in COBOL, divisions and sections.

Within each unit:

Group all data entry tasks together.

Group all calculations and processing together.

Group all data display tasks together.

Whether you are dealing with a subroutine or procedure or a block of code within a main program, for readability your code should have the form

data entry tasks

data manipulation and
calculation tasks

data display tasks

The following BASIC program shows this grouping concept.

```
10 REM THIS PROGRAM SORTS NUMERICAL INPUT
```
Data entry (input)
```
20 PRINT "HOW MANY ITEMS DO YOU WANT SORTED";
30 INPUT N
40 DIM X(N)
50 FOR M = 1 TO N
60     INPUT X(M)
70 NEXT M
```
Data manipulation (processing)
```
80 FOR K = 1 TO N - 1
90     FOR J = K + 1 TO N
100         IF X(K) = X(J) THEN 140
110         LET T = X(K)
120         LET X(K) = X(J)
130         LET X(J) = T
140     NEXT J
150 NEXT K
```
Data display (output)
```
160 FOR L = 1 TO N
170     PRINT X(L);
180 NEXT L
999 END
```

Systematize for readability

(See reference 11.)

Don't trade readability for efficiency.

Don't make optimization your main concern.

Consider carefully the relations among the modules you have written. Organize the modules so that you are not displaying results prematurely or attempting to process information that has not yet been entered. Hand-trace your modules (and then the program as a whole) to see that nothing is being done before or after its time.

Efficiency is certainly a major element in the evaluation of any program. However, what good is an "efficient" program that nobody can read or understand? If you tinker with the program to make it more efficient, don't decrease the program's readability in doing so. This warning holds especially for large production programs that need to be both efficient and readable. If the program becomes unreadable at any point, the people maintaining this software will have difficulties modifying it. Unreadable programs are inefficient because they waste expensive programmer time.

Your main concern is to write lucid, readable code. If you succeed in this task, optimization will follow. Optimization benefits not only machines but also people, because unoptimized programs can be plodding and frustrating for the user. (This problem is especially true of on-line processing utilities such as data-based query systems that managers use to get up-to-date information about their business.)

REFERENCES

1. Carma L. McClure, "Top-Down, Bottom-Up, and Structured Programming," *IEEE Transactions on Software Engineering,* vol. SE-1, no. 4, December 1975, pages 397 – 403.

2. Edsger W. Dijkstra, "Notes on Structured Programming," in *Structured Programming* by O.-J. Dahl, E. W. Dijkstra, and C. A. R. Hoare, Academic Press, New York, 1972, pages 1 – 82.

3. Jean Dominique Warnier, *Logical Construction of Programs,* Van Nostrand Reinhold, New York, 1976.

4. Stanley Gill, "Thoughts on the Sequence of Writing Software," in *Software Engineering—Concepts and Techniques,* edited by J. N. Buxton, Peter Naur, and Brian Randell, Petrocelli/Charter, New York, 1976, pages 116 – 118.

5. Clement L. McGowan and John R. Kelly, *Top-Down Structured Programming Techniques,* Petrocelli/Charter, New York, 1975.

6. Edward F. Miller Jr. and George E. Lindamood, "Structured Programming: Top-Down Approach," *Datamation,* vol. 19, no. 12, December 1973, pages 55 – 57.

7. H. Mills, "Top-Down Programming in Large Systems," in *Debugging Techniques in Large Systems,* edited by Randall Rustin, Prentice-Hall, Englewood Cliffs, N.J., 1971, pages 41 – 55.

8. J. B. Dennis, "Modularity," in *Software Engineering—An Advanced Course,* edited by F. L. Bauer, Springer-Verlag, Berlin, 1973, pages 128 – 182.

9. J. Maynard, *Modular Programming,* Auerbach Publishers, Princeton, N.J., 1972.

10. Russell M. Armstrong, *Modular Programming in COBOL,* John Wiley & Sons, New York, 1973.

11. Ned Chapin, "Aids to Producing Comprehensible Software," in *Structured Programming* (Infotech State of the Art Report), Infotech International Ltd., Maidenhead, Berkshire, U.K., 1976, pages 165 – 181.

USE DECISION AND REPETITION STRUCTURES

Cecil's dispatch of business was extraordinary, his maxim being, "The shortest way to do many things is to do only one thing at once."

Samuel Smiles, Self-Help

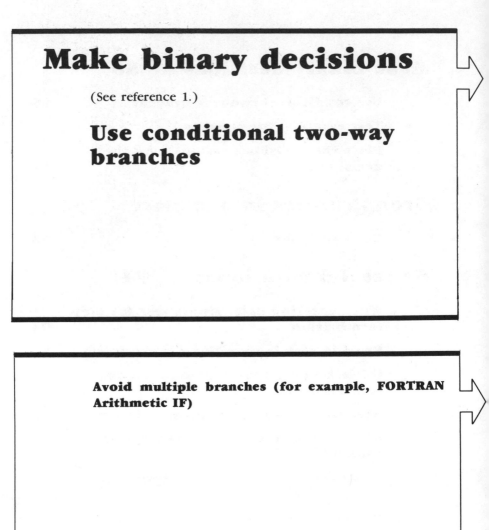

Make binary decisions

(See reference 1.)

Use conditional two-way branches

Avoid multiple branches (for example, FORTRAN Arithmetic IF)

There are only three basic decision structures. They are:

1 IF (expression) THEN (statement or branch)

2 IF (expression) THEN (statement or branch)
                      ELSE (statement or branch)

3 multiple decision structure, such as FORTRAN's
IF (expression) Statement No., Statement No., Statement No.

Of the above three structures, 1 and 2 are essentially the same. Structure 1 is a special case of the more general structure 2, since it is equivalent to

IF (expression) THEN (statement or branch)
                  ELSE (do nothing)

Multiple branches often are hard to trace and may yield erroneous results. The general form of the arithmetic IF is

$$\text{IF (expression) } S_1, \quad S_2, \quad S_3$$

where transfer of control is to S_1 if the expression is evaluated as negative, to S_2 if it is evaluated as zero, and to S_3 if it is evaluated as positive. The zero test may yield unexpected results if you are not careful. If your expression involves only integers, then the zero test may be reliable. However, if your expression involves real numbers, for example,

$$\text{IF (expression) } 10, 20, 30$$

then the zero test probably will fail. The expression may never be *exactly* zero because of round-off errors. This error may be very small, but it will prevent the expression from ever becoming zero, and hence it may make the program branch incorrectly. Such errors are very difficult to detect, so the best idea is to avoid them by not using multiple branches.

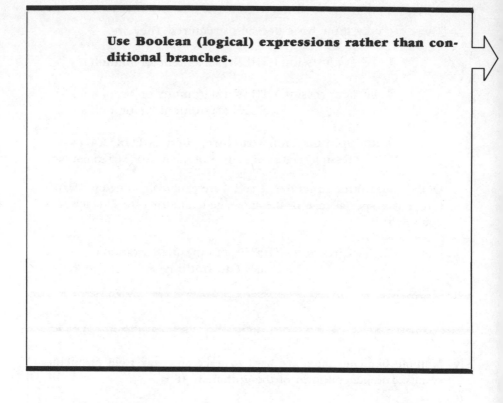

Use Boolean (logical) expressions rather than conditional branches.

Test carefully for equality

(See reference 2.)

Don't use real (floating point) numbers in the test.

Don't forget that 10.0*0.1 may not always equal 1.0 exactly.

conditional expression	may be rewritten as a simple expression
if X *then* Y *else* Z	$(X.AND.Y).OR.(.NOT.X.AND.Z)$
if A *then* true *else* false	A
if A *then* false *else* true	.NOT.A
if A *then* true *else* true	*true*
if A *then* false *else* false	*false*
if A *then* true *else* B	A.OR.B
if A *then* false *else* B	.NOT.A.AND.B
if A *then* B *else* true	.NOT.A.OR.B
if A *then* B *else* false	A.AND.B

The simple logical expressions given on the right are preferable to the conditional expressions on the left. Each logical expression requires only one (instead of two) evaluations. Thus the simple expression accomplishes the same goal for roughly half the computation cost.

When dealing with real numbers, we also have to deal with possible round-off errors. These errors may cause incorrect final results, and therefore equality should be tested with integers. Errors also accumulate in repetitive arithmetic. For example,

$$.1 + .1 + .1 + .1 + .1 + .1 + .1 + .1 + .1 + .1 \neq 10.0 * 0.1$$

As we add the first two terms, we accumulate a round-off error in conversion from internal representation to decimal representation. With each addition, the error increases, and the final result may be unpredictable.

Place the decision's actions near the decision

Group choices in one place

Do it by cases

(See references 3, 4, 5, 6.)

Prevent unnecessary branching by grouping the decision's actions together whenever appropriate.

In COBOL we are allowed to nest IFs as follows:

```
IF  MALE  THEN
     IF  MARRIED  THEN
          ADD  1  TO  MARRIED—MALES
                    ELSE
          ADD  1  TO  SINGLE—MALES
          ELSE

     IF  MARRIED  THEN
          ADD  1  TO  MARRIED—FEMALES
                    ELSE
          ADD  1  TO  SINGLE—FEMALES .
```

Although several languages allow nested IFs of the form IF ... THEN IF ..., it is not generally a good idea to use this construct. It is difficult for humans to trace through such a construct and even more difficult to keep track when writing the program segment of the ELSEs.

ALGOL W and PASCAL allow the use of a generalized conditional statement called the CASE statement.

Do it by cases

(continued)

Isolate the choices near the selection mechanism.

Be careful with loops

(See references 7, 8.)

When entering data, always test for loop termination

This IF statement

> IF (Boolean expression) THEN (statement)
> ELSE (statement)

also can be expressed with the CASE statement as follows:

> CASE (Boolean expression) OF
> *true* : (statement);
> *false* : (statement)

This construct allows us to group our choices near the decision point. Other languages have similar constructs.

The *effect* of a certain choice should not be so distant from its *cause* as to be difficult or impossible to find. You should be able to answer the questions "Where does this choice lead?" and "Where does this choice come from?"

Loops are an indispensable programming device, because repetition in some form is the fundamental reason behind most programs. However, don't risk the embarrassment of uncontrolled repetition. Just as heating machines require thermostats, programs with loops need loop-end checks.

Test for loop termination with a trailer (marker) or by End Of File.

This test is extremely important if you are dealing with an unknown number of data items. For example,

```
100 READ X
110 IF X = -1 THEN 300
120 DATA 53, 67, 81, . . ., 55, 41, -1
130 . . .
    .
    .
    .
200 GO TO 100
    .
    .
    .
300 . . .
```

The marker (−1) saves you the trouble of having to count the data and makes sure that data entry stops correctly.

In FORTRAN you can terminate either at the end of the list or wherever there is an erroneous item anywhere in the list. For example,

```
    READ (6, 100, ERR=200, END=500)
100 FORMAT (5X, 10F6.2)
    .
    .
    .
C.....INCORRECT DATA ITEM FOUND
200 ....
    .
    .
    .
C.....LIST COMPLETELY READ
500 ...
```

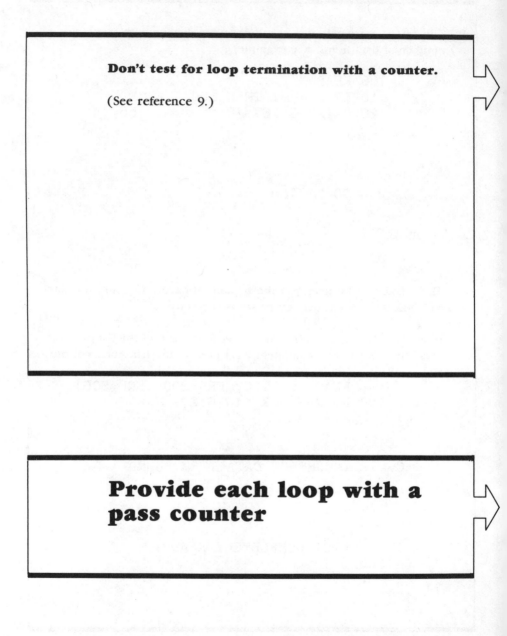

Don't test for loop termination with a counter.

(See reference 9.)

Provide each loop with a pass counter

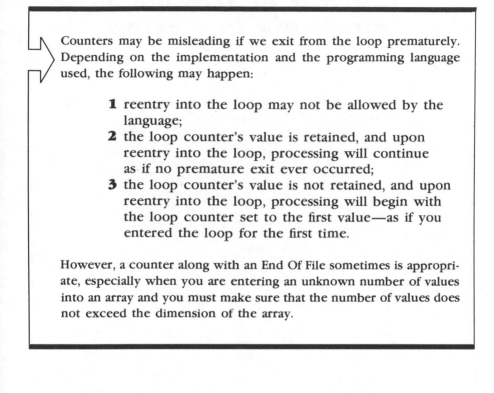

Counters may be misleading if we exit from the loop prematurely. Depending on the implementation and the programming language used, the following may happen:

1 reentry into the loop may not be allowed by the language;

2 the loop counter's value is retained, and upon reentry into the loop, processing will continue as if no premature exit ever occurred;

3 the loop counter's value is not retained, and upon reentry into the loop, processing will begin with the loop counter set to the first value—as if you entered the loop for the first time.

However, a counter along with an End Of File sometimes is appropriate, especially when you are entering an unknown number of values into an array and you must make sure that the number of values does not exceed the dimension of the array.

Often it is important when you are debugging a program to know how many times your program processed a certain loop. If you have a loop counter, you know exactly how many times you have processed the loop at that point in the program.

Initialize or zero out all ac-cumulators just before the loop

Do not initialize or zero out accumulators within a loop.

Respect the loop by treating it as a unit

(See reference 10.)

```
10 LET X = 0 ←──────────── { initialized X prior to entry
                            { into FOR–NEXT loop
20 FOR I = 1 TO 5
30    LET X = X + I * 2 ←─{ used X as an accumulator

40    PRINT X; ←────────── { results are
                           { 2  6  12  20  30
50 NEXT I
60 END
```

However, the above program will not work correctly if we insert the initialization within the loop:

```
10 FOR I = 1 TO 5
20    LET X = 0 ←────────── { initialization within the loop

30    LET X = X + I * 2 ←─{ used X as an accumulator

40    PRINT X; ←────────── { results are
                           { 2  4  6  8  10
50 NEXT I
60 END
```

In general, initialize as close to the loop as possible all variables that you will be using as accumulators within the loop. Thus you will be sure that the variables are initialized even though the same variables may have been used somewhere else in the program.

Consider the loop as one of your modules. Test it and debug it separately from the other modules so that it performs its tasks as a module correctly. Make the loop a self-contained unit: leave the loop only after you have completed everything within the loop. Do not depend on outside decisions and information for the loop.

Take care not to allow jumps into the inside of a
loop.

Respect the loop variable as a special, controlled object

(See reference 11.)

Do not modify the loop variable's value within the
loop.

Do not depend on the loop variable for calculations
outside the loop. Always transfer the loop variable's value to another variable if you need its value
outside the loop.

The loop should be a self-contained module: your program should not require a premature exit from the loop or an entrance into it from some other portion of the program. In many cases, a jump into a loop generates a run-time error. However, in some languages that allow jumps into the inside of a loop, results are unpredictable. Avoid having to decipher them!

Although most languages seem either to ignore changes of loop variables within loops or to restrict such changes, changing loop variables yields unpredictable results from one implementation to another. For example, in PASCAL,

```
X := 10;
FOR I := 1 TO X DO
     BEGIN
     .  .  . ;
     X := X + 1
     END
```

the loop will execute only 10 times and will ignore the change to the final value of the loop variable. This same program segment will execute differently in some of the ALGOLs.

Upon loop termination, the value of the controlled variable in a FORTRAN DO loop generally is not the variable's last value used inside the loop before the loop was left. After control leaves the body of the loop, in most versions of PASCAL and some versions of ALGOL the loop variable is left undefined. In some versions of BASIC the loop variable value may linger for the duration of the program after exit from the loop. Results are unpredictable from one implementation to another.

Don't reevaluate the same expression within a loop

Evaluate expressions once, outside the loop.

Keep the number of expression evaluations within a loop to a minimum.

Expressions needing only one evaluation should be placed outside of loops. It is wasteful to reevaluate the same expression each time for the duration of the loop. The reason for including loops in programs is to speed up calculations. By enclosing computations that only require one evaluation inside a loop, we are misusing the loop structure.

Bad

```
 5 LET X = Y = 11
10 FOR I = 1 TO 100
20    LET X = Y + 5 * (Y + 7)
30    LET J = J + I
40    PRINT J
50 NEXT I
60 PRINT X
70 END
```

Good

```
 5 LET X = Y = 11
10 LET X = Y + 5 * (Y + 7)
20 LET J = 0
25 FOR I = 1 TO 100
30    LET J = J + I
40    PRINT J
50 NEXT I
60 PRINT X
70 END
```

Do not overlap inner loops with outer loops

(See references 12, 13.)

Place inner loops completely within the outer loops.

For most languages that allow nested loops, the allowable nestings are the following:

$$\left[\left[\left[\quad \text{or} \quad \left[\left[\left[\quad \text{or} \quad \left[\left[\left[\right.\right.\right.\right.\right.\right.$$

The following nestings are not allowed:

$$\left[\left[\left[\quad \text{or} \quad \left[\left[\left[\quad \text{or} \quad \left[\left[\left[\right.\right.\right.\right.\right.\right.$$

An analogy can be made between nesting loops and stacking bowls or boxes. If we were to attempt to put a smaller bowl within a larger bowl, we would succeed. However, the other way around would not work. Similarly, let us say we have a large box and several smaller boxes. The larger box can contain the smaller boxes, but only in a specific order: first the large box, followed by the boxes of the next size, which will in turn contain boxes of smaller size, and so on. We cannot "stack" these boxes: they all must fit within each other.

Nest loops sparingly

Resist the urge to stuff your program with clever multiply nested loops.

Avoid writing programs that have this structure:

```
┌ FOR ...
│   ┌ FOR ...
│   │   ┌ FOR ...
│   │   └ NEXT ...
│   └ NEXT ...
│   ┌ FOR ...
│   └ NEXT ...
│   ┌ FOR ...
│   └ NEXT ...
└ NEXT ...
```

Programs with multiply nested loops are very difficult to trace and debug. Your program may be doing unnecessary extra work. The nesting may not be correct and results will be unpredictable. The program will be slow and costly.

REFERENCES

1. Dennie Van Tassel, *Program Style, Design, Efficiency, Debugging, and Testing* (2nd edition), Prentice-Hall, Englewood Cliffs, N.J., 1978, pages 147–150.

2. Brian W. Kernighan and P. J. Plauger, *The Elements of Programming Style* (2nd edition), McGraw-Hill Book Company, New York, 1978, page 116.

3. Joan K. Hughes and Jay I. Michtom, *A Structured Approach to Programming,* Prentice-Hall, Englewood Cliffs, N.J., 1977, pages 67–70.

4. C. A. R. Hoare, "Case expressions," *ALGOL Bulletin,* No. 18, October 1964, pages 20–22.

5. Barth C. Wrandle, "Notes on the CASE Statement," *Software—Practice and Experience,* vol. 4, no. 3, July–September 1974, pages 289–298.

6. W. C. M. Vaughan, "Another Look at the CASE Statement," *SIGPLAN Notices,* vol. 9, no. 11, November 1974, pages 32–36.

7. Dennie Van Tassel, *Program Style, Design, Efficiency, Debugging, and Testing* (2nd edition), Prentice-Hall, Englewood Cliffs, N.J., 1978, pages 142–147.

8. C. A. R. Hoare, "A Note on the FOR Statement," *BIT,* vol. 12, no. 3, 1972, pages 334–341.

9. Shmuel Katz and Zohar Manna, "A Closer Look at Termination," *Acta Informatica,* vol. 5, no. 4, 1975, pages 333–352.

10. W. W. Peterson, T. Kasami, and N. Tokura, "On the Capabilities of WHILE, REPEAT, and EXIT Statements," *Communications of the ACM,* vol. 16, no. 8, August 1973, pages 503 – 512.

11. William Wulf and Mary Shaw, "Global Variable Considered Harmful," *SIGPLAN Notices,* vol. 8, no. 2, February 1973, pages 28 – 34.

12. Marilyn Bohl, *Tools for Structured Design,* Science Research Associates, Chicago, 1978, pages 25 – 37 and 49 – 60.

13. George Ledin Jr., *A Structured Approach to General BASIC,* Boyd & Fraser Publishing Co., San Francisco, 1978. See Chapter 13 ("Repeating"), pages 135 – 168.

8

SPLIT YOUR PROGRAM INTO SUBPROGRAMS

Learn to live, and live to learn,
Ignorance like a fire doth burn,
Little tasks make large return.

Bayard Taylor, To My Daughter

Divide and conquer   114

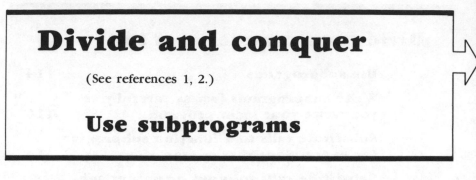

Divide and conquer

(See references 1, 2.)

Use subprograms

Limit each subprogram to one task.

(See reference 3.)

Limit the length of each subprogram to a screenful or pageful.

A subprogram is a self-contained set of program statements designed to perform a specific task. It is awkward and difficult to trace a program composed entirely of single statements. It is also wasteful to write the same code over and over every time you need to calculate the same thing.

A subprogram should do one thing well. If it takes too long, revise it.

Write subprograms just as carefully as you write your main program

(See reference 4.)

Prevent trouble.

Write subprograms that are independent.

Make sure that your subprograms recognize and can recover from incorrect data.

(See references 5, 6, 7.)

Make each subprogram complete in all the details it would need if it were run by itself. Avoid making subprograms dependent on other subprograms. Retain the flexibility of being able to use a particular subprogram in another context, for another application.

Write subprograms that will handle spurious, incomplete, incompatible, and missing data.

Substitute often-appearing expressions with calls to a function subprogram

(See reference 8.)

Suppose you need to calculate the polynomial

$$1 + X + X ** 2 + X ** 3 + X ** 4$$

many times in your program for different values of X. You could
write the following program:

```
 10 LET A = 3
 20 LET B = 1 + A + A**2 + A**3 + A**4

100 LET G = 7
120 LET H = 1 + G + G**2 + G**3 + G**4

200 LET X = 127
220 LET Y = 1 + X + X**2 + X**3 + X**4
```

Or you could save yourself the trouble of typing the line every time
(and having to check it for correctness!) and write the following
program:

```
 10 DEF FNA(Z) = (((Z + 1)*Z + 1)*Z + 1)*Z + 1
 20 LET A = 3
 30 LET B = FNA(A)

100 LET G = 7
120 LET H = FNA(G)

200 LET X = 127
220 LET Y = FNA(X)
```

or

```
 10 DEF FNA(Z) = (((Z + 1)*Z + 1)*Z + 1)*Z + 1
 30 LET B = FNA(3)
120 LET M = FNA(7)
220 LET Y = FNA(127)
```

Substitute often-appearing data entry or data display program segments with calls to input or output sub-routines

Avoid recursion unless iteration makes the subprogram less readable

Your program does some calculations and then needs to print some tables and graphs based on the results of the computations. This cycle may be repeated many times throughout your program. It is wasteful to include the required output statements every time you need to use them. Separate the output routine from the rest of the program and put it in a subprogram. Since the subprogram can be tested separately for correctness, there will be less chance of making a mistake. Also, the main program will be less cluttered with diverse statements and thus will be easier to trace and debug.

Iteration and recursion are two fundamental forms of repetition. *Iteration* is simple repetition, in which a certain calculation is carried out more than once. *Recursion* means "curving back on itself" or "bootstrapping."

Not all languages allow recursion. Iteration may be more machine efficient, but recursion often is more natural. If you can do a task with either recursion or iteration, compare the two approaches.

Recursive procedure

```
int proc FACTORIAL(n);
     int value n;
     FACTORIAL :=
        if n < 0
           then − MAXINT
           else if n = 0
                   then 1
                   else n*FACTORIAL(n−1);
```

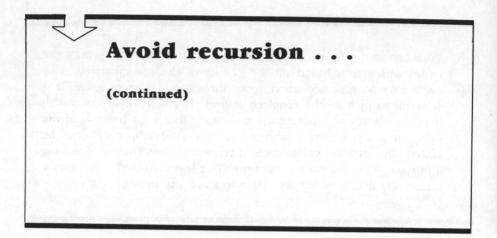

Avoid recursion . . .

(continued)

Use recursive subprograms for recursive data structures only.

(See references 9, 10, 11.)

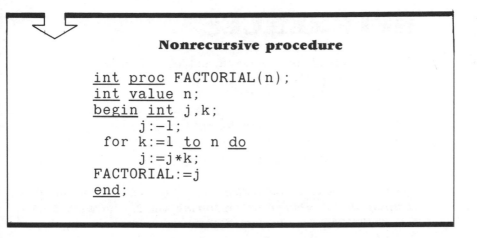

Nonrecursive procedure

```
int proc FACTORIAL(n);
int value n;
begin int j,k;
      j:-1;
  for k:=1 to n do
      j:=j*k;
FACTORIAL:=j
end;
```

Languages such as PASCAL, ALGOL, PL/1, APL, and SIMULA allow recursive data structures. LISP is the premier example of a recursive language. Use the recursive features of a language for which it is designed.

REFERENCES

1. Alfred V. Aho, John E. Hopcroft, and Jeffrey D. Ullman, *The Design and Analysis of Computer Algorithms,* Prentice-Hall, Englewood Cliffs, N.J., 1974, pages 60–65.

2. Ellis Horowitz and Sartaj Sahni, *Fundamentals of Computer Algorithms,* Computer Science Press, Potomac, Md., 1978. See Chapter 3 ("Divide-and-Conquer"), pages 98–151.

3. George Polya, *Mathematical Discovery—On Understanding, Learning, and Teaching Problem Solving*, vol. 2, John Wiley & Sons, New York, 1965. See Chapter 8 ("Plans and Programs") and Chapter 9 ("Problems Within Problems"), pages 22–53.

4. John Rhodes, "Tackle Software with Modular Programming," *Computer Decisions,* vol. 5, no. 10, October 1973, pages 21–25.

5. Peter Naur, "Programming by Action Clusters," *BIT,* vol. 9, no. 3, 1969, pages 250–258.

6. Gerhard Goos, "Hierarchies," in *Software Engineering—An Advanced Course,* edited by F. L. Bauer, Springer-Verlag, Berlin, 1973, pages 29–46.

7. Ole-Johan Dahl and C. A. R. Hoare, "Hierarchical Program Structures," in *Structured Programming* by O.-J. Dahl, E. W. Dijkstra, and C. A. R. Hoare, Academic Press, New York, 1972, pages 175–220.

8. Frank L. Friedman and Elliot B. Koffman, *Problem Solving and Structured Programming in FORTRAN,* Addison-Wesley Publishing Co., Reading, Mass., 1977. See Chapter 7 ("Subprograms"), pages 237–286.

9. D. W. Barron, *Recursive Techniques in Programming* (2nd edition), Macdonald/American Elsevier, London, 1975.

10. William H. Burge, *Recursive Programming Techniques,* Addison-Wesley Publishing Co., Reading, Mass., 1975.

11. C. A. R. Hoare, "Recursive Data Structures," *International Journal of Computer and Information Sciences,* vol. 4, no. 2, June 1975, pages 105 – 132.

9

BE CAREFUL WITH VARIABLES AND EXPRESSIONS

Mr. Hannaford's utterances have no meaning; he's satisfied if they sound clever.

Alfred Sutro, The Walls of Jericho

Initialize variables before using them   128

Choose meaningful variable names   136

Use the same variables often   140

Parenthesize expressions for clarity   142

Initialize variables before using them

(See reference 1.)

Do not let the system initialize your program's variables by default.

A variable is not defined until it has been declared (that is, assigned with a type) *and* initialized (that is, assigned with a value).

Variables are program objects that hold values for the duration of a program. These values are allowed to change at any point in the program. Since a variable *holds* a value, it must have a beginning or initial value. Some language implementations do the initialization of variables automatically, usually to zero. However, many language versions do not initialize variables. Rather than gamble on what the system will or will not do for you, assign the values *you* want to each variable before using the variables. Most languages provide convenient ways to initialize variables. In COBOL you can place values into a whole table. In FORTRAN you can use the DATA statement, as follows:

$$DATA\ I,J,K/1,2,3/$$

which is equivalent to

```
I = 1
J = 2
K = 3
```

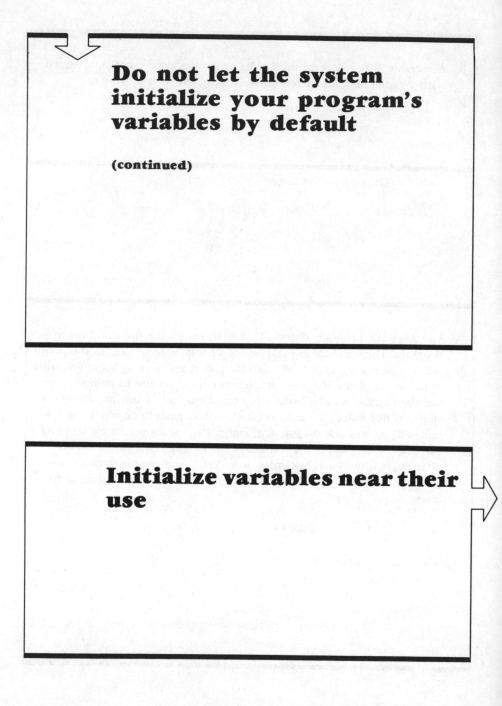

Do not let the system initialize your program's variables by default

(continued)

Initialize variables near their use

In BASIC you can initialize variables quickly to a single value with a multiple assignment statement:

```
10 LET A = B = C = D = ... = Z = 0
```

or in a loop

```
100 FOR I = 1 TO 1000
150 READ A(I)
160 RESTORE
200 NEXT I
300 DATA 0
```

By controlling the values held by the variables in your program, you minimize unexpected errors caused by surprise initializations by the system.

Unless the language has declarative statements that allow wholesale initialization, there is no need to initialize all variables at the beginning of your program if you are not going to use them all at once, and as long as all those variables to be used in a well-defined segment of the program are initialized locally in that segment. A simple exception is the DATA statement in FORTRAN.

If an error does occur, it is easier to trace a program that has a modular structure (and hence has changes in variable and initializations all in one program area) than one that has variables scattered all over it.

**Do not initialize variables with declarative state-
ments.**

Do not initialize at the point of declaration.

How much do you save with something like

$$\underline{\text{int}} \text{ TWENTYFIVE=25;}$$

or

$$\underline{\text{real}} \text{ PI := 3.14159265; ?}$$

Certainly PI is a convenient shorthand, but the number 25 itself obviously is to be preferred over any other representation. COBOL has *figurative constants,* which are reserved words that stand for specific numbers of literals. The figurative constant ZERO (and its plurals, ZEROES or ZEROS) represents the number 0.

A program clause called a *declaration* is used in programming languages to relay information to the compiler or translator about the properties associated with the data to be held by the variables. Declarations may provide the following information about the variables:

1 their type (real, integer, boolean, string, and so on),
2 size of the arrays.

Languages such as LISP, APL, BASIC, and SNOBOL4 do not use explicit declarations. Other languages such as ALGOL, PASCAL, COBOL, FORTRAN, and PL/1 require declarations. Declarations enhance the readability of your program by providing it with "bookkeeping".

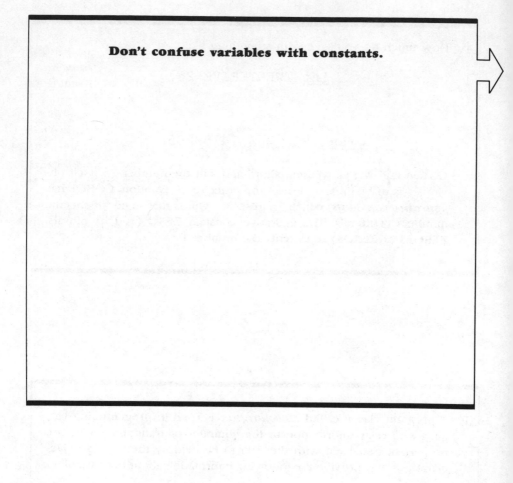

Don't confuse variables with constants.

A variable is an object that holds, represents, or stands for, another object, never itself. Variables also are called *pointers* or *references* because they "point to" or "refer to" values. These values may change during the execution of the program. A numeric variable represents (or holds) a number, a string variable holds a string (a linear array of characters), and a boolean or logical variable holds "true" or "false." Variables therefore are *identifiers* of values. In most languages, names or strings of letters and digits beginning with a letter are acceptable as variables. Thus, SUM, BALANCE, CLIENTS, and RMP942 are examples of variables. Different rules hold for different languages, however. Most languages impose a limit on the length of the name (on the number of characters comprising the name). Six-character to eight-character names are usual in FORTRAN, and single letter, letter-digit, and letter-dollar sign are the variable names in most versions of BASIC. More liberal rules apply in the ALGOLs and in COBOL.

A constant is an object that is itself and does not represent any other object. Constants can be numeric, string, or logical, and they do not change during the execution of the program. Constants do not change because a 2 cannot be a 3, a B cannot be a C, and *"true"* cannot be *"false."*

Choose meaningful variable names

(See references 2, 3, 4, 5.)

Find names that are descriptive of the variables' purposes.

Avoid acronyms or mnemonics.

Avoid obscure or cute names or abbreviations.

Although some languages, such as BASIC, do not allow variables to take on names other than one letter or a letter followed by a number, most other languages allow longer variable names. The purpose of the following expression is not clear because the variables are single letters.

$$R = D * .174533E-01$$

However,

$$RADIAN = DEGREES * .174533E-01$$

immediately makes the expression understandable: we are converting from degrees to radians. The intermediate form of this expression

$$RDN = DGR * 174533E-01$$

is not as clear as the one in which the variable names were completely written out. Six- to eight-character variable name lengths may be maximum in the language you are using, unless you are using COBOL, which has liberal English-like naming facilities and allows names to be from one to 30 characters long and to consist of letters, digits, and hyphens. Examples of COBOL names are:

```
EMPLOYEE-NUMBER
SOCIAL-SECURITY-NUMBER
PAYROLL3-CHECK
FICA-RATE
WITHHOLDING-SCHEDULE24
```

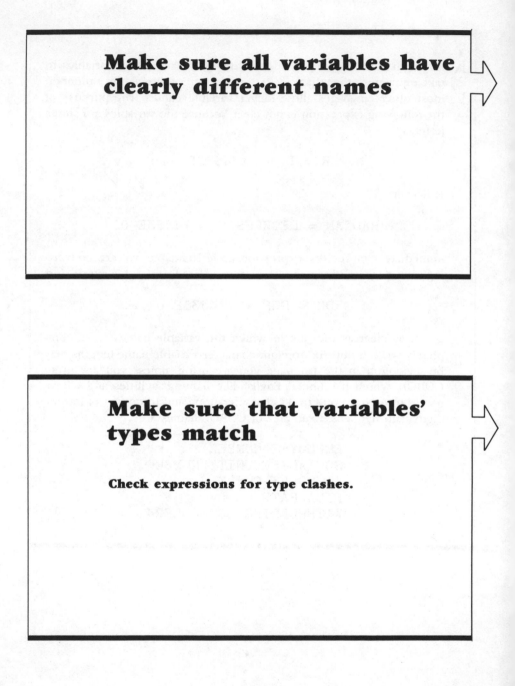

Make sure all variables have clearly different names

Make sure that variables' types match

Check expressions for type clashes.

The difficulty in debugging a large program that utilizes many variables is having to keep track of variables with names like B or B1 or B10. For example,

```
B = B + B1 - B10 * 10 - 1 - B1/10
```

If our program has many such expressions, it is very easy to make a mistake in either the formula or the checking. A good rule to remember when creating variable names is to make each name different by at least two characters, preferably at the beginning of the name. This way the program and the programmer will be less error prone and the resulting program will be more readable.

Many common errors occur when mixed-mode expressions are evaluated. For example,

```
ISUM = SUM/IDIFF
```

In FORTRAN, ISUM is integer, and so is IDIFF, but SUM is real. The result of SUM/IDIFF will be truncated, and only the highest possible integer will be stored in ISUM. Hence, inaccuracies in the result may influence the rest of the program. Be careful of truncation. More important, do not confuse simple and array variables of the same type or variables of different types (logical, numeric, string, and so on). Mixed-mode difficulties most probably will be identified during compile time.

Use the same variables often

Make sure that each variable will appear more than once in a program structure.

Be careful with temporary (intermediate) variables

(See reference 6.)

If the variable appears only once in a program structure, then it serves no purpose and can be removed. A single appearance must be a mistake: either the variable only stores data, in which case the data clearly are inaccessible, or the variable serves to output data, in which case it is either impossible to do so or potentially very confusing. Although two appearances by a variable may mean you have avoided such a mistake, you always should minimize the number of variables used. The fewer the variables, the less storage is needed by your program. Use each variable as often as you can. Think of variables as limited resources, as you would think of registers.

Temporary variables are unavoidable and indispensable only in program segments in which value interchanges occur. Everywhere else, temporary variables are better avoided. Why clutter your program with additional objects? Why use up additional memory space?

Parenthesize expressions for clarity

(See reference 7.)

Use parentheses for quality control

Use redundant parentheses to ensure that expressions are evaluated the way you intended.

(See reference 8.)

Do not rely on precedence rules.

Although arithmetic operator precedence is always the same in most programming languages—exponentiation first; multiplication and division second, from left to right; and addition and subtraction third, from left to right—parentheses have the highest priority. All expressions within parentheses are evaluated before any other. Suppose we have the following formula:

$$A = B + C - D ** E/F * G$$

The precedence rules would evaluate it as if the formula were

$$A = ((B + C) - (((D ** E)/F) * G))$$

but perhaps what you wanted was

$$A = ((B + C - D) ** (E/F)) * G$$

or perhaps

$$A = B + ((C - D) ** (E/(F * G)))$$

The cost of compiling extra parentheses is more than worthwhile for clarity. So use redundant parentheses if they improve clarity and readability.

Use parentheses to improve the expressions' readability.

Use parentheses to facilitate error checking.

Write a particular expression only once

Never recompute what already has been computed.

When debugging your program, you may easily make a mistake while evaluating an expression. If that expression is parenthesized, then the only precedence rule you need to evaluate it correctly is:

Begin with the innermost parentheses and evaluate expressions there, working your way outwards.

The more readable the expression, the less likely it is that an error will occur. Of course, you still need to know whether the language you are using evaluates expressions from left to right (for example, FORTRAN, COBOL, BASIC) or from right to left (for example, APL).

Do not force the computer to evaluate an expression more than once. Suppose your program has the following expressions:

```
INTO = A * B - ((SCORE1 + SCORE2)/2) - 17
OPT = C * ((SCORE1 + SCORE2)/2) ** 2
```

Your program is reevaluating (SCORE1 + SCORE2)/2 each time, although the rest of the expression is different. A better way is

```
AVE = (SCORE1 + SCORE2)/2
```

Then change the other expressions to

```
INTO = A * B - AVE - 17
OPT = C * AVE ** 2
```

This makes each expression more readable, and AVE need be evaluated only once.

REFERENCES

1. Brian W. Kernighan and P. J. Plauger, *The Elements of Programming Style* (2nd edition), McGraw-Hill Book Co., New York, 1978. See Chapter 6, page 101.

2. Anthony J. Guttmann, *Programming and Algorithms: An Introduction,* Heinemann Educational Books, London. See Chapter 6 ("Programming Style and Practice"), pages 120 – 121.

3. G. Michael Schneider, Steven W. Weingart, and David M. Perlman, *An Introduction to Programming and Problem Solving with PASCAL,* John Wiley & Sons, New York, 1978, page 76 (Style Clinic 3-4).

4. Michael Jackson, "Mnemonics," *Datamation,* vol. 13, no. 4, April 1967, pages 26 – 28.

5. Edward Yourdon, *Techniques of Program Structure and Design,* Prentice-Hall, Englewood-Cliffs, N.J., 1975. See Chapter 1 ("The Characteristics of a 'Good' Computer Program"), pages 21 – 22.

6. Henry F. Ledgard, *Programming Proverbs,* Hayden Book Co., Rochelle Park, N.J., 1975, pages 29 – 31.

7. Dennie Van Tassel, *Program Style, Design, Efficiency, Debugging, and Testing* (2nd edition), Prentice-Hall, Englewood Cliffs, N.J., 1978, pages 23 – 24.

8. Clark Weissman, *LISP 1.5 Primer,* Dickenson Publishing Co., Belmont, Calif., 1967, pages 43 – 44. The careful use of parentheses is particularly important in a language like LISP!

AVOID INDISCRIMINATE JUMPS

She jumps about like a flea on a blanket.

Aristophanes, The Fleas

Execute sequentially   150

Watch out for erroneous jumps   156

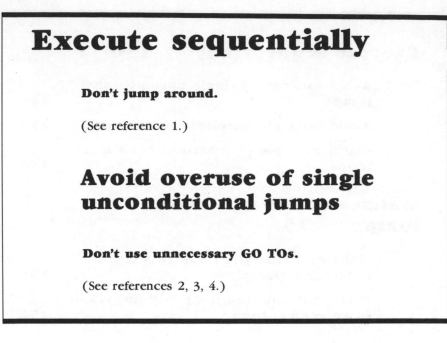

Execute sequentially

Don't jump around.

(See reference 1.)

Avoid overuse of single unconditional jumps

Don't use unnecessary GO TOs.

(See references 2, 3, 4.)

Avoid multiple unconditional jumps

Don't use unnecessary computed GO TOs.

One obvious structure for transfer of control in programming languages is the single unconditional jump, or the GO TO. It also is one of the most abused control structures. Heavy use of the GO TO in programs makes them difficult to read, debug, trace, and maintain. In a program that has labeled statements (as in BASIC, COBOL, FORTRAN, or even ALGOL), transfer of control may be made to a certain statement from many different segments of the program. It is cumbersome to trace the program and keep track of all the unconditional jumps. To do so, one must scan the whole program. For example, if in tracing a program you reach a group of GO TO statements, control may go off in various directions, and you may not be able to determine easily the relationship of these various program paths. If you trace only one path and ignore all the others, you may reach further jumps or decisions and perhaps never return to the original transfer of control area.

The use of FORTRAN's computed GO TO or ALGOL 60's switch or of FORTRAN's assigned GO TO or BASIC's multiple unconditional jump may lead to problems in program tracing. The transfer of control depends on some index variable, as in

FORTRAN

```
GO TO (100,200,300,400,500), I
```

BASIC

```
ON I GOTO 100,200,300,400,500
```

or

```
GOTO I OF 100,200,300,400,500
```

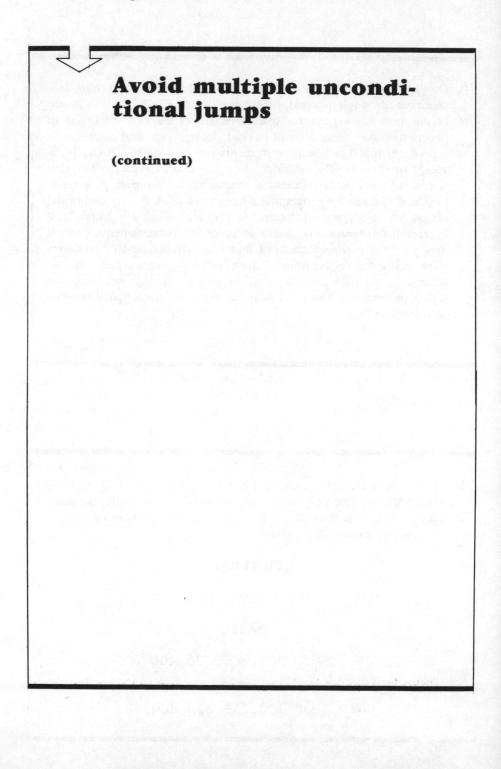

Avoid multiple unconditional jumps

(continued)

So, if I = 1, then the program branches to 100; if I = 2, then it branches to statement labelled 200; and so on. In FORTRAN, the assigned GO TO takes the form

GO TO N, (100,200,300,400)

where somewhere in the program we have ASSIGN 300 TO N. Since the destination of the jump is determined elsewhere in the program, the exact result of the decision (the jump destination) is difficult to establish without a hand trace of the entire program. In COBOL, the ALTER command allows dynamic changing of transfer of control.

We could say

Al. GO TO Bl.

and then later have

ALTER Al TO PROCEED TO B2.

The ALTER command changes the destination of the GO TO statement. Thus, a program may execute differently each time it is run, and this difference may even involve the original program logic. The language implementor's goal is to generate optimized executable code. Optimization depends on the control structures present in a program.

When GO TOs and labels are used liberally throughout the program, the compiler must do a lot of work to analyze the control structure before optimizing. Thus, the presence of needless jumps is costly and may make optimization impossible. Whenever possible, program as sequentially as possible. Use subprograms to minimize your need to jump around. However, don't write unclear, awkward code in an effort to avoid GO TOs. Don't sacrifice clarity or a straightforward program so that you can claim to have written a "GO TO-less" program!

Avoid multiple (premature) exits from loops

(See reference 5.)

One of the most undetectable mistakes a programmer can make is to create a loop that contains a GO TO statement jumping outside the body of the loop. The results can be unpredictable from one version of a programming language to another. Problems arise not only from jumps out of a loop, but also from jumps back in if jumping back in is allowed! Similarly, unpredictable results can be created by jumps from or into blocks or sections of code such as subroutines or subprograms. (Again, we assume that such jumps are legal or pass undetected at run time.) Since in BASIC the subroutine is not separated from the main program, it somehow must be bypassed. One usually can avoid it with a STOP statement or a GO TO statement. For example,

```
10 DIM . . .                        10 DIM . . .
20 . . .                            20 . . .
40 GOSUB 200                             .
50 . . .                                 .
        .               or          40 GOSUB 800
        .                           50 . . .
190 GOTO 310                             .
200 FOR I = . . .                        .
220 PRINT . . .                     310 . . .
240 GOTO 400 ─────┐                      .
        .         │                      .
        .         │ Premature exit  400 . . . ◄──────┐
        .         │                      .           │ Premature exit
300 RETURN        │                      .           │
310 . . .         │                 790 STOP         │
        .         │                 800 FOR I = . . .│
        .         │                 820 PRINT . . .  │
        .         │                 840 GOTO 400 ────┘
400 . . . ◄───────┘                      .
        .                                .
        .                           900 . . .
999 END                             999 END
```

Watch out for erroneous jumps

(See references 6, 7, 8.)

Make sure that you jump to a legally executable statement

Never jump to other jump statements.

Never jump into loops and subprograms.

(See references 9, 10, 11.)

Make sure that the jump will not result in an endless loop

(See reference 12.)

Do not jump to another unconditional jump command. Watch out for self-referencing jumps.

Check all labels to see that the statement to which you are jumping is correctly labeled. Although most compilers will either warn you of your misuse of the jump instructions or halt the execution of your program, you should not depend on the compiler to weed out your mistakes. Many language implementations do not have extensive error-checking facilities. Hence, a statement sequence such as

```
1000 GO TO 2000
    . . .            hundreds of statements
    . . .            in between
       .
2000 GO TO 1000
```

may go undetected. In most cases, unconditional jumps are the cause of such endless loops. Jumping into loops or subroutines causes unpredictable results.

If you are using the FORTRAN computed GO TO, do not use labels that refer to other GO TOs.

```
100 GO TO (50,120,300,350), I
  .
  .
  .
120 GO TO (60,100,300,340), J
```

Although such absurdities as

```
500 GO TO 500
```

"can't happen", unbelievable as it may seem, occasionally they do happen. Watch out!

Don't write programs that will not stop by them-selves.

(See reference 13.)

Don't involve the operator in the normal running of your program by the user.

Provide your program with checks to determine whether you are supplying the correct amount of data. Don't let your program default to system errors such as

PROGRAM OUT OF DATA AT STATEMENT X

or perhaps

PRINT SPECIFICATIONS EXCEEDED AT LINE X

Your program should stop elegantly even in the absence of data or in the presence of bad data. Tell the user of your program what the limitations of your program are. Then make sure that your program can be used with the correct limitations or boundary conditions by providing error-checking routines that prevent either overflow or system defaults.

By providing error-checking routines, you allow your program to "fail softly." If the user provides data that will cause your program either to yield a bewildering message or to enter an endless loop that can be stopped only by the operator, then your program is not doing the proper job. Don't assume that the user never will enter such data! Create a good edit check for all input data. Then test your program thoroughly before making it available to the public.

REFERENCES

1. Edsger W. Dijkstra, "GOTO Statement Considered Harmful," *Communications of the ACM,* vol. 11, no. 3, March 1968, pages 147 – 148, 538, 541.

2. Donald Ervin Knuth and Robert W. Floyd, "Notes on Avoiding 'GO TO' Statements," *Information Processing Letters,* vol. 1, no. 1, February 1971, pages 23 – 31, 177.

3. B. M. Leavenworth, "Programming with(out) the GOTO," in *Proceedings of the ACM Annual Conference,* Boston, August 1972, pages 782 – 786.

4. Calvin E. Elgot, "Structured Programming With and Without GO TO Statements," *IEEE Transactions on Software Engineering,* vol. SE-2, no. 1, March 1976, pages 41 – 54.

5. R. V. Evans, "Multiple Exits from a Loop Using Neither GO TO nor Labels," *Communications of the ACM*, vol. 17, no. 11, November 1974, page 650.

6. Donald Ervin Knuth, "Structured Programming with GOTO Statements," *Computing Surveys,* vol. 6, no. 4, December 1974, pages 261 – 301.

7. Peter Naur, "GO TO Statements and Good ALGOL Style," *BIT,* vol. 3, no. 3, 1963, pages 204 – 208.

8. Edward Ashcroft and Zohar Manna, "The Translation of 'GO TO' Programs to 'While' Programs," in *Proceedings of the IFIP Congress 1971,* vol. 1, North-Holland Publishing Co., Amsterdam, 1972, pages 250 – 255.

9. Daniel M. Berry, "Loops with Normal and Abnormal Exits," *Modeling and Measurement Note 23*, Computer Science Department, University of California, Los Angeles, 1974.

10. G. V. Bochmann, "Multiple Exits From a Loop Without the GOTO," *Communications of the ACM,* vol. 16, no. 7, July 1973, pages 443 – 444.

11. D. Pager, "Some Notes on Speeding Up Certain Loops by Software, Firmware, and Hardware means," *IEEE Transactions on Computers,* vol. C-21, no. 1, January 1972, pages 97 – 100.

12. N. H. Weiderman and B. H. Rawson, "Flowcharting Loops Without Cycles," *SIGPLAN Notices,* vol. 10, no. 4, April 1975, pages 37 – 46.

13. Clinton R. Foulk, "The DO Trace: A Simple and Effective Method for Debugging GOTO-free Programs," *SIGPLAN Notices,* vol. 10, no. 9, September 1975, pages 11 – 18.

11

CODE AND DEBUG YOUR PROGRAM

In spring, trap the bugs by placing refuse turnip or cabbage leaves in the garden, then destroy the bugs attracted to them.

Richard H. Cravens, Pests and Diseases

Code carefully   164

Debug intelligently   168

Code carefully

(See reference 1.)

Be on the lookout for orthographic errors (typos)

Some of the most frustrating mistakes one can make are orthographic. Orthographic errors are spelling, spacing, or formatting mistakes. Here are some rules to guide you:

1 In algorithmic languages, be sure your blocks have beginnings and endings. In languages such as ALGOL and PASCAL, each *begin* should have a matching *end*. In the C language, each { (left curly brace) should have a matching } (right brace). In LISP, be sure that in your expressions, the number of left parentheses is equal to the number of matching right parentheses. In BASIC, each GOSUB must have a matching RETURN and each FOR must have a matching NEXT. In FORTRAN, be sure your WRITEs or PRINTs and READs have appropriate matching FORMATs and the DO statement has a matching CONTINUE or other allowed statement correctly labeled. Although the language's compiler will catch and flag these omissions, it will do so usually and frustratingly at run time.

2 When entering or displaying information, be sure that you are providing adequate formats. Avoid inelegant program termination and messages like "PROGRAM OUT OF DATA" by entering or displaying only what is available. Use the EOF (End-Of-File) test for termination. Not all programming languages have EOF, and few work the same way. Check your system's manuals to find the correct way to use the End-Of-File concept.

3 Avoid spelling mistakes by proofreading your program before running it. Check all your variable, constant, subprogram, and file names to see that they are spelled correctly and consistently throughout the program. Watch for simple spelling mistakes such as FORNAT instead of FORMAT (in FORTRAN).

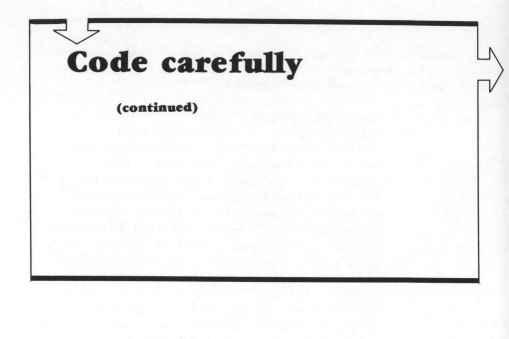

Code carefully

(continued)

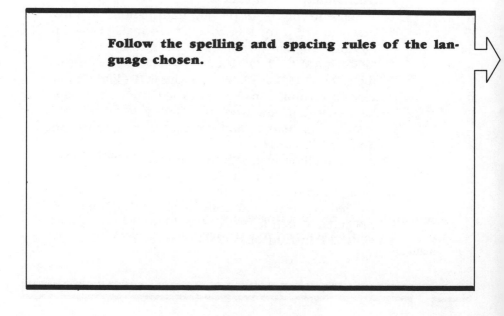

Follow the spelling and spacing rules of the language chosen.

4 Be sure you are using the appropriate job control language to get your program to execute.

5 Know the kind of parameter passing mechanism that your programming language is using so that you get the results you want from your subroutincs and procedures.

6 Determine the limitations of your programming language. If you are using a three dimensional array, find out if your language or the implementation you are using allows it. Every feature that you want may not be available on the machine you are using. Is the library function or routine you plan to use available on your system?

Never assume that because a library routine or function is called one way in one language, the same routine will have the same name in another language. Although SIN and COS are used in most languages, the routine that generates random numbers or the routine that calculates the square root of a number often are given different names. For example, in FORTRAN the routine that calculates the square root is called SQRT; in BASIC it is SQR; while in PASCAL, SQR *squares* the numbers and SQRT obtains the *square root*! Many languages ignore blank lines and spaces. So a GO TO can be written (in a language such as BASIC, FORTRAN, or PASCAL) as GO TO or GOTO or even G OT O without any run-time penalties. However, the program may be hard to read, and in a language such as SNOBOL4 a blank space is an operator! Whenever you are not sure, check your system's manuals.

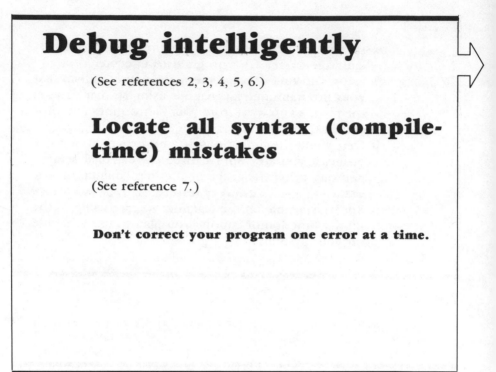

Debug intelligently

(See references 2, 3, 4, 5, 6.)

Locate all syntax (compile-time) mistakes

(See reference 7.)

Don't correct your program one error at a time.

Use debugging aids

(See references 8, 9, 10, 11, 12.)

Favor debugging compilers.

Although many compilers provide adequate error messages, especially when the language is misused, it is a good idea to check other locations in the program where the error may have had some impact. Some language implementations stop on the first error and do not search further. In those cases, you are provided with only one instance of an error. Hand-trace your program to find all others.

It is a wasteful practice to correct one error and rerun the program in the hope that after several runs, all the errors will be caught by the computer and the program will work. Not only is this practice costly, but unless your system has excellent error messages and error-checking capabilities, many subtle errors go unnoticed.

However, some syntax errors are masked by previous ones and are truly difficult to detect, so multiple compilations may be needed. Since the cost of people effort is higher than the cost of machines (that is the reason for automation, or as IBM said, "Machines should work, people should think"), let the compiler go at it once more. Meanwhile, take a break!

If debugging compilers are available, run your programs on them, because they yield clearer error messages and pointers to trouble spots, provide summaries of variable usage, and summarize results of subroutines or procedures. With the more complete information provided by this type of compiler, your job of ridding your program of bugs will be much easier.

Know your error messages.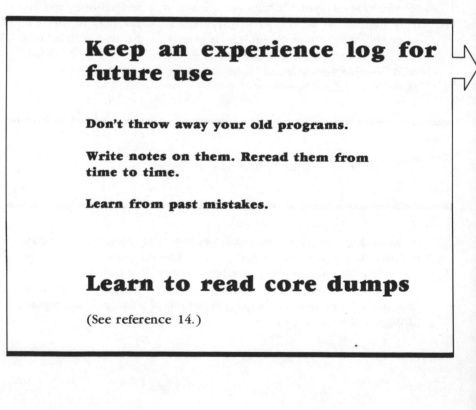

Keep an experience log for future use

Don't throw away your old programs.

Write notes on them. Reread them from time to time.

Learn from past mistakes.

Learn to read core dumps

(See reference 14.)

Get a list of error messages common to your system. If no such list exists, write one yourself by jotting down the error message and the cause in a notebook. Use pretty printers (automatic indenting and column aligning software), if available. Not only will your program be more appealing to the eye, but finding its errors and inconsistencies will be considerably easier. (See reference 13.)

Keep track of all your corrections. Keep at least one copy of the original program when running the corrected version. If your corrections yield worse results, at least you have the previous version to return to. Otherwise you have no record of the changes you have made to the program. Don't rely on your memory—write changes down!

Keep the final runs of your programs and document them with information as to

1 how you obtained the solution and what errors occurred along the way,
2 corrections that you introduced that did not work,
3 a summary of what you learned in the process of developing this program.

Refresh your memory periodically by looking through your old programs.

Make changes carefully to avoid introducing new errors

(See reference 15.)

REFERENCES

1. C. R. Litecky and G. B. Davis, "A Study of Errors, Error-proneness, and Error Diagnosis in COBOL," *Communications of the ACM,* vol. 19, no. 1, January 1976, pages 33–37.

2. A. R. Brown and W. A. Sampson, *Program Debugging—The Prevention and Cure of Program Errors,* Macdonald/American Elsevier, London, 1973.

3. Randall Rustin (editor), *Debugging Techniques in Large Systems* (Courant Computer Science Symposium 1, 1970), Prentice-Hall, Englewood Cliffs, N.J., 1971.

4. R. S. Gaines, "The Debugging of Computer Programs," Ph. D. Thesis, Princeton University, Princeton, N.J., 1969.

Trace errors backward to their source. Has the error affected other sections of your program? Make sure that the changes you make are consistent with the rest of the program. Hand-trace the resulting program: Does it do what you expect it to do?

Make sure that you have not forgotten to do anything and that in making the changes you have not left out statements or whole sections of code that were in the original run. Do the changes introduced affect your program's data entry or data display sections? When doing this, refer to high-level documentation, such as program HIPO, to ensure that all impacts have been reviewed.

5. J. D. Gould, "Some Psychological Evidence on How People Debug Computer Programs," *International Journal of Man-Machine Studies,* Vol. 7, no. 2, March 1975, pages 151 – 182.

6. Ben Shneiderman and Don McKay, *Experimental Investigations of Computer Program Debugging and Modification,* Computer Science Department, Indiana University, Bloomington, Ind., Technical Report No. 48, April 1976.

7. Stephen J. Boies and John D. Gould, "Syntactic Errors in Computer Programming," *Human Factors,* vol. 16, no. 3, May – June 1974, pages 253 – 257.

8. T. G. Evans and D. L. Darley, "DEBUG—An Extension to Current On-Line Debugging Techniques," *Communications of the ACM,* vol. 8, no. 5, May 1965, pages 321 – 326.

9. P. C. Poole, "Debugging and Testing," in *Software Engineering—An Advanced Course,* edited by F. L. Bauer, Springer-Verlag, Berlin, 1973, pages 278–318.

10. R. L. van Steeg, "TALK—A High Level Source Language Debugging Technique," *Communications of the ACM,* vol. 7, no. 7, July 1964, pages 418–419.

11. E. Satterthwaite, "Debugging tools for High Level Languages," *Software—Practice and Experience,* vol. 2, no. 3, July–September 1972, pages 197–218.

12. Edward Yarwood, *Toward Program Illustration,* Computer Systems Research Group, University of Toronto, Toronto, Technical Report CSRG-84, October 1977.

13. Henry F. Ledgard, *Programming Proverbs,* Hayden Book Co., Rochelle Park, N.J., 1975, pages 42–43.

14. Daniel H. Rindfleisch, *Debugging System 360/370 Programs Using OS and VS Storage Dumps,* Prentice-Hall, Englewood Cliffs, N.J., 1976.

15. Robert T. Nicholson, "Debugging Your Program," *Personal Computing,* vol. 2, no. 4, April 1978, pages 22–24.

12

TEST AND EDIT
YOUR PROGRAM

Bring me to the test.

Shakespeare, Hamlet

Test your program

(See references 1, 2, 3, 4, 5, 6, 7, 8.)

Test-run your program in segments

Test each segment separately.

Test the data entry segment with carefully chosen and representative data

Set up actual (ordinary) conditions.

Program testing is a later stage of debugging. The purpose of testing is to validate the correctness of a program, that is, to make sure that it performs according to specifications.

Make your programs modular (split them into separate segments or subprograms). Test each block as you would a separate program. Combine the blocks and test the entire program. How is each segment affected by

      1 ordinary data,
      2 bad data,
      3 a combination of good and bad data?

Make sure that each segment has safeguards to prevent the processing of unusual or bad data.

When entering data, display it before any processing has been done so that you can see that it has been entered correctly. This point is especially important if your data is coming from a random number generator. You do not *see* the data as it is generated, so you should display it in order to inspect it. Make sure that your data entry code segments handle the expected data efficiently.

Correct all the logic mistakes

Run the program with traces if you have to.

Insert output statements in each segment to be traced.

Design your program to handle exceptions

Test your program with borderline data

(See references 9, 10.)

Try out extreme or unusual data.

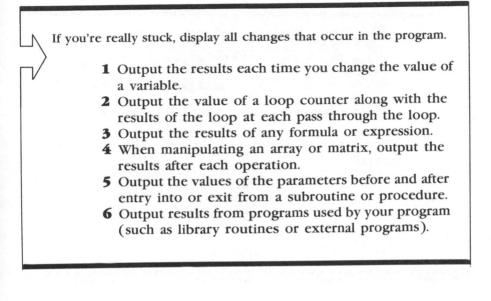

If you're really stuck, display all changes that occur in the program.

1 Output the results each time you change the value of a variable.
2 Output the value of a loop counter along with the results of the loop at each pass through the loop.
3 Output the results of any formula or expression.
4 When manipulating an array or matrix, output the results after each operation.
5 Output the values of the parameters before and after entry into or exit from a subroutine or procedure.
6 Output results from programs used by your program (such as library routines or external programs).

Test your program with bad data. Your program

1 should not stop processing because of bad data,
2 should screen all data and process only the good data,
3 should output the bad data and display a message explaining why it was not suitable,
4 should not transfer control to the operating system or the system programmer so as to "catch all the bad input."

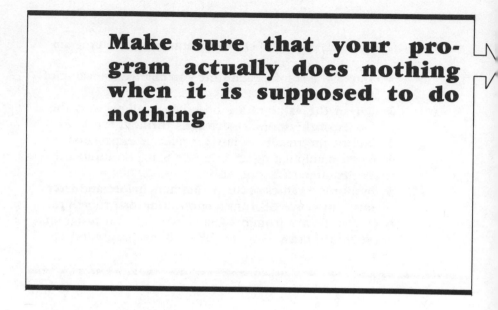

Make sure that your program actually does nothing when it is supposed to do nothing

Edit your program

(See reference 11.)

Rewrite

Don't be satisfied with your rough draft just because it runs.

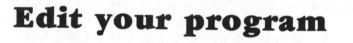

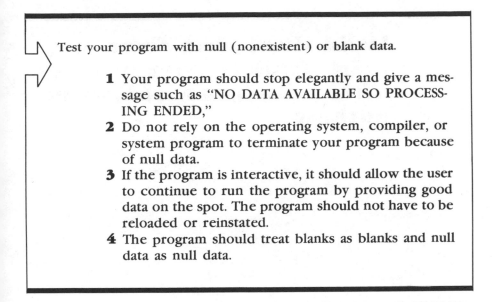

Test your program with null (nonexistent) or blank data.

1 Your program should stop elegantly and give a message such as "NO DATA AVAILABLE SO PROCESSING ENDED,"
2 Do not rely on the operating system, compiler, or system program to terminate your program because of null data.
3 If the program is interactive, it should allow the user to continue to run the program by providing good data on the spot. The program should not have to be reloaded or reinstated.
4 The program should treat blanks as blanks and null data as null data.

Many a program luckily runs because

1 it was tested only with selected data,
2 it has no obvious flaws,
3 only the author can run it. He or she is the only person who understands how the program works.

Replace lucky runs with dependable runs. A practical way to test a run is with randomly generated data that resembles what really will be used. Beware of the rapidly put together "working" program: it may "work" solely because it has yet unobserved bugs!

Avoid short-term fixes

Don't take the easy way out by patching.

Favor clarity over efficiency

Don't just change the program here and there. If a clear program using your original method of solution is inefficient, start over with a better method.

After you have corrected your program, answer these questions:

1 Is the program sequential?
2 Is each program segment well documented?
3 Is the program easy to read and easy to understand?
4 Is the output from the program easy to read and easy to understand?
5 Does the program handle ordinary data along with null data and bad data?
6 Does the program use variables efficiently?
7 Does the program run as quickly and efficiently as possible?

If the answer to any one of these questions is "no," rewrite until you can answer "yes."

If after each run you must make corrections, change the requirements for the data, or rewrite large sections, you should search for a better method to solve the problem. A bad algorithm or method or program generally

1 works when you least expect it,
2 puts unnecessary constraints on the user,
3 only works for carefully selected input,
4 outputs confusing results,
5 is not sequential,
6 makes you take too much time to discover what is wrong with it,
7 causes a new error to surface each time you test it,
8 may run fast, but probably does not run at all.

Remember that to be good, an algorithm does not have to be clever, hard to understand, or even optimal. *If you do not understand what an algorithm is supposed to do, don't use it!*

Prove your program correct

Prove the correctness of the program text.

(See references 12, 13, 14, 15, 16.)

If it is available, use an automatic program ver-ifier.

(See references 17, 18, 19.)

REFERENCES

1. William C. Hetzel (editor), *Program Test Methods,* Prentice-Hall, Englewood Cliffs, N.J., 1973.

2. J. C. Huang, "An Approach to Program Testing," *Computing Surveys,* vol. 7, no. 3, September 1975, pages 113–128.

3. David J. Panzl, "Test Procedures: A New Approach to Software Verification," in *Proceedings of the 2nd International Conference on Software Engineering* (October 13–15, 1976, San Francisco), IEEE Press, New York, pages 477–485.

Few applications programs need to be subjected to rigorous proofs. A wealth of experience with a particular well tested program is often enough. However, a new program that implement's a new method can benefit from a formal demonstration of correctness because it is ordinarily impractical to test all possibilities, and sometimes it may be impossible to ascertain why the method should work at all.

Verifiers for research are available. Commercial program-verifying packages are coming into the market. Request a demonstration. Keep up with the literature.

4. Edward F. Miller Jr., "Program Testing: Art Meets Theory," *Computer,* vol. 10, no. 7, July 1977, pages 42 – 51.

5. John B. Goodenough, "Program Testing Survey," in *Infotech State-of-the-Art Report,* 1977.

6. James C. King, "A New Approach To Program Testing," in *Proceedings of the 1975 International Conference on Reliable Software,* April 1975, Los Angeles, pages 228 – 233. Also in *SIGPLAN Notices,* vol. 10, no. 6, June 1975, pages 493 – 510.

7. James C. King, "Symbolic Execution and Program Testing," *Communications of the ACM,* vol. 19, no. 7, July 1976, pages 385 – 394.

8. John A. Darringer and James C. King, "Applications of Symbolic Execution to Program Testing," *Computer,* vol. 11, no. 4, April 1978, pages 51–60.

9. John B. Goodenough and Susan L. Gerhart, "Toward a Theory of Test Data Selection," *IEEE Transactions on Software Engineering,* vol. SE-1, no. 2, June 1975, pages 156–173.

10. Richard A. DeMillo, Richard J. Lipton, and Frederick G. Sayward, "Hints on Test Data Selection: Help for the Practicing Programmer," *Computer,* vol. 11, no. 4, April 1978, pages 34–41.

11. E. A. Youngs, "Error-Proneness in Programming," Ph. D. Thesis, University of North Carolina, Chapel Hill, N.C., 1971.

12. Edsger W. Dijkstra, "Structured Programming," in *Software Engineering—Concepts and Techniques,* edited by J. N. Buxton, Peter Naur, and Brian Randell, Petrocelli/Charter, New York, 1976, pages 222–226.

13. Sidney L. Hantler and James C. King, "An Introduction to Proving the Correctness of Programs," *Computing Surveys,* vol. 8, no. 3, September 1976, pages 331–353.

14. Suad Alagić and Michael A. Arbib, *The Design of Well-Structured and Correct Programs,* Springer-Verlag, New York, 1978.

15. Robert B. Anderson, *Proving Programs Correct,* John Wiley & Sons, New York, 1979.

16. C. A. R. Hoare, "Proof of a Program: FIND," *Communications of the ACM,* vol. 14, no. 1, January 1971, pages 39–45.

17. L. P. Deutsch, "An Interactive Program Verifier," Ph. D. Thesis, Department of Computer Science, University of California, Berkeley, Calif., 1973, and Xerox PARC Report CSL-73-1, Palo Alto, Calif.

18. D. I. Good, R. L. London, and W. W. Bledsoe, "An Interactive Program Verification System," *IEEE Transaction on Software Engineering,* vol. SE-1, no. 1, April 1975, pages 59–67.

19. Susan L. Gerhart, *Program Verification in the 1980s: Problems, Perspectives, and Opportunities,* Information Sciences Institute, University of Southern California, Marina Del Rey, Calif., Report ISI/RR-78-71, August 1978.

13

UTILIZE SOFTWARE TOOLS

Handle your tools without mittens.

Benjamin Franklin, Poor Richard's Almanac, 1758

Use library (packaged) functions   192

Use commercial packages   194

Use library (packaged) functions

(See references 1, 2, 3, 4, 5.)

Learn these functions' idiosyncracies

Don't reinvent the wheel, but don't assume that library functions are always correct.

Look through your computer center's manuals to see what are the available library functions. Write short programs that test these routines. Keep notes on each library program you use. Refer to these notes when you intend to use the packaged functions. Find out which library functions are available with which language. Plan your input data to be in a form acceptable to the library function. What do the results produced by these functions look like?

Check the accuracy of the results by looking at published tables. See where a round-off mistake may change the results. Make notes on how much decimal-place accuracy you can expect to get from numeric functions. Test string library functions to determine whether any information is lost in the conversion. Remember that EBCDIC and ASCII collating sequences are different. Write your own routines only if

1 there are no programs that do what you need done;
2 there is nothing published in the computing literature either;
3 there are available library routines, but you need much greater accuracy or speed.

Keep track of all your experiences. Keep copies of your programs that either use library functions or have subprograms written by you that do a better job than the library functions. Refer to them when you need to write similar programs. If commercial or other packaged software is unavailable, build your own library.

Use commercial packages

(See references 6, 7, 8.)

Familiarize yourself with your computer center's program library

Keep up with software developments

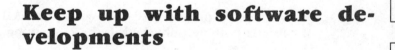

Get the manuals that are available in your computer center and read them. Take notes about their usefulness to you. For those that are directly useful for your applications, test and run sample programs to discover their idiosyncracies. Keep a log of your experiences with these program packages. Rate them on the following traits:

1 ease of use (simple to understand and use, awkward, difficult),
2 ease of interfacing with other programs,
3 readability of results generated by the program,
4 documentation accompanying the package,
5 accuracy of the results generated by the program,
6 cost of using the package and running time.

Check your computer center library for magazines and journals that describe new software developments. Commercial magazines like *Datamation* often rate and review new software packages: this information may be very helpful. Check journals in your research area for published algorithms.

REFERENCES

1. Brian W. Kernighan and P. J. Plauger, *Software Tools,* Addison-Wesley Publishing Co., Reading, Mass., 1976.

2. John W. Pomeroy, "A Guide to Programming Tools and Techniques," *IBM Systems Journal,* vol. 11, no. 3, 1972, pages 234 – 254.

3. Richard L. Sites, "Programming Tools: Statement Counts and Procedure Timings," *SIGPLAN Notices,* vol. 13, no. 12, December 1978, pages 98 – 101.

4. Marilyn Bohl, *Tools for Structured Design,* Science Research Associates, Chicago, 1978.

5. Ron Lane, *An Introduction to Utilities,* Petrocelli/Charter, New York, 1975.

6. Andries van Dam and David E. Rice, "On-Line Text Editing: A Survey," *Computing Surveys,* vol. 3, no. 3, September 1971, pages 93 – 114.

7. W. R. Schucany, B. S. Shannon Jr. and P. D. Minton, "A Survey of Statistical Packages," *Computing Surveys,* vol. 4, no. 2, June 1972, pages 65 – 79.

8. Richard W. Moore, *Introduction to the Use of Computer Packages for Statistical Analyses,* Prentice-Hall, Englewood Cliffs, N.J., 1978.

9. A good source for information on new software is the magazine *ICP INTERFACE, Data Processing Management,* published by International Computer Programs, Indianapolis, Ind.

14

EVALUATE YOUR PROGRAM'S PERFORMANCE

His promises were, as he then was, mighty;
But his performance, as he is now, nothing.

Shakespeare, Henry VIII

Measure the times involved   200

Measure the times involved

(See references 1, 2, 3, 4.)

Keep track of the time it took you to produce the program

Add program development, testing, coding, and debugging times.

1 When developing the algorithm and program, note down how long it took you to find the algorithm. Did you find it in the literature or use a software package? Where did you locate this prewritten program? If you developed the algorithm yourself, did you use flowcharts or decision tables?

2 When testing your algorithm, how long did it take you to trace the algorithm with good data, bad data, and a mixture of good and bad data? Did the algorithm work in all cases?

3 When coding the algorithm, how long did it take you to translate your algorithm into a suitable programming language? Were there any difficulties that could have been avoided?

4 When tracing through the coded algorithm, how long did it take you to trace the program with good data, bad data, and a mixture of good and bad data? Did the algorithm work in all cases?

5 When debugging your program after the initial run, how long did it take you to spot the errors? How long did each error take to correct? Which corrections were easiest to insert? If you needed to rewrite sections of code, how long did it take you to find an alternative method, code it, test it, and rerun the program? If the data was not representative, how long did it take you to choose adequate data to test your program?

Make the compile time of your program as short as you can

(See references 5, 6, 7, 8, 9.)

Measure your program's execution times for several different jobs

Measure your program's input/output time for a variety of typical jobs

Compile time is a measure of the time it takes the compiler to translate your program. This time often is difficult to minimize, so whenever possible you should use good optimizing compilers. Follow the rules in this book to write straightforward and nonredundant code.

Often you can get information on execution time of your program by requesting it on one of your job control cards. Also, you can put counters inside loops and routines (some languages have the CLOCK or TIME functions) to measure the activity of the program as it runs. Study these results as a profile of the program's execution. Use this information to guide optimization efforts, but *don't do it at the expense of clarity.*

Among the important things to measure are

1 How many cards or lines of code were read?
2 What was the ratio of imperative to declarative statements?
3 How many pages or screenfuls were displayed?
4 How much magnetic tape or disk time was used?
5 How many cards or how much paper tape was punched?
6 How much plotter or other peripheral time was used?

REFERENCES

1. Tom Gilb, *Data Engineering,* Studentlitteratur, Stockholm, 1976.

2. Robert M. Graham, "Performance Prediction," in *Software Engineering—An Advanced Course,* edited by F. L. Bauer, Springer-Verlag, Berlin, 1973, pages 395−463.

3. C. C. Gotlieb, "Performance Measurement," in *Software Engineering—An Advanced Course,* edited by F. L. Bauer, Springer-Verlag, Berlin, 1973, pages 464−491.

4. Tom Gilb, *Software Metrics,* Winthrop Publishers, Cambridge, Mass., 1977.

5. Domenico Ferrari, "The Improvement of Program Behavior," *Computer,* vol. 9, no. 11, November 1976, pages 39−47.

6. Paul J. Jalics, "Improving Performance the Easy Way," *Datamation,* vol. 23, no. 4, April 1977, pages 135−148.

7. H. C. Lucas, Jr., "Performance Evaluation and Monitoring," *Computing Surveys,* vol. 3, no. 3, September 1971, pages 79−91.

8. F. E. Allen, "Program Optimization," in *Annual Review in Automatic Programming,* vol. 5, 1969, Pergamon Press, New York, pages 239−307.

9. Domenico Ferrari and Edwin Lau, "An Experiment in Program Restructuring for Performance Enhancement," in *Proceedings of the 2nd International Conference on Software Engineering* (October 13−15, 1976, San Francisco), IEEE Press, New York, pages 146−150.

15

ANNOTATE AND DOCUMENT YOUR PROGRAM

I wish he would explain his explanation.

Lord Byron, Don Juan

Write an explanation for each major program segment   208

Explain briefly   208

Write an explanation for each major program segment

(See reference 1.)

Explain briefly

Use comments only where necessary.

Choose the right comment form

(See references 2, 3.)

Complete the thought begun by the code.

At the beginning of each program segment, provide comments that explain

    1 what algorithm you are using and what it is like,
    2 what is the significance of each variable,
    3 what results are expected.

You may also need to describe the algorithm itself, especially if you are its author.

Don't annotate each statement or explain the obvious. At the beginning of your program, provide a segment of comments that explains your program thoroughly. Then at each block of computations, at each input and output block, and in each subroutine or procedure, explain what the block of code does in relation to the rest of the program. Use comments to clarify the code, not merely to rewrite it. An arbitrary but good rule of thumb is to have one line of comments for each 10 to 20 lines of code.

Make the code read like a book. Consider the beginning block of comments as a summary of the plot and characters. In the subsequent blocks of comments, describe the scene changes and plot twists in detail. Reread the comments after you have written them. If they are not clear to you, rewrite them until they are. Continue refining the comments until you stop asking yourself "Now, what did I mean by that?" If you are unable to write clear comments, perhaps the code itself is poor and won't lend itself to a clear explanation. Even if you think it's clear, have another programmer read your code and comments to locate unclear parts, just in case.

Don't hide comments in the code by placing comments on the same line with code.

Don't wedge comments between statements on the same line.

Many programming languages allow more than one statement per line as long as these statements are separated by some delimiter such as a colon (as in some versions of BASIC) or semicolon (as in the ALGOLs, in PL/1 and its variants, and in PASCAL). Don't force the reader to distinguish the code from the comments, besides trying to understand what you are doing! Here is an example of a PASCAL program segment that wedges comments everywhere:

```
begin (*We have to read the dimensions of the ma-
trix here*)
READLN(M,N);(*Now we print the error message if
 the following condition is met*)if (M<1)or(N>
 10)or(N<1)or(M>10)then WRITELN ('Dimensions
 are incorrect') else begin (*We now read one line
 of input at a time*)
                         etc....
```

Clear comments appear separated from the code. The clearest comments appear not only separated, but also framed: for example,

```
******************************************
*                                        *
*                                        *
*                                        *
*      SUBPROGRAM TO CALCULATE           *
*                                        *
*                                        *
*                                        *
*      YIELD RATIOS AT THE DATE OF       *
*                                        *
*                                        *
*                                        *
*      MATURITY OR SURRENDER             *
*                                        *
*                                        *
******************************************
```

Do not rely on the output for program annotation.

Display major annotations prominently

Segregate all major comments from the program segments to which they are directed.

Use blank comment lines as separators.

Although your output should be thoroughly documented, it should not be your program's only documentation. What if your program for some reason does not work and the user wishes to discover why? Because your program will provide no guidance, the user will be confronted by nothing except code, and will have to trace through your program and document it. Who needs this drudgery and pain? Let us further suppose that the user is *you,* looking at the code a year or more later. Your program does not work ... then *you* will have to reanalyze the whole program to find out what is wrong! However, if you had put in comments, the job would have been much easier. Don't rely on your memory for documentation—it is easier and more dependable to write your comments down!

COBOL programmers can insert explanations in their program's procedure division with the statement

```
NOTE THIS SECTION CALCULATED
THE EFFECTIVE DISCOUNT RATE.
```

where the reserved word NOTE signals the beginning of a comment. Elsewhere in the COBOL program the programmer can insert explanations on any line by writing an asterisk in column 7 as follows:

```
123456*---DISCOUNT RATE CALCULATIONS
```

Each language has its own explicit comment facility. In BASIC, programmers can write REM statements (or maybe even resort to unreferenced image statements). In FORTRAN, the letter C in column 1 makes the remaining 79 columns into a comment.

Write a reference manual

(See references 4, 5, 6, 7.)

Describe what you did and how you did it

Help yourself and other programmers to update and alter the program in the future

List the tests and debugging aids that you used in writing the program

Give a detailed description of the algorithm you used. If the algorithm or program is not original, provide its source, author, version level, and machine environment considerations (storage, files, operating system, and so on). Explain not only *how* you wrote the program and what it does, but also *why* it was a necessary program. Also explain whether the program did what you expected it to do, and what areas may need improvement. Explain which portions of the program are general and which require a specific kind of input. Explain the limitations of the program. What is the largest problem that it will solve? What is the smallest?

Also include your (programmer's) name, affiliation, date of release, version level (if applicable), and machine environment considerations, such as storage, file handling, and operating system requirements.

Reproduce in the manual the program's runs of these tests.

Specify the system's requirements

State what hardware, operating system, and file management are required and what other resources are to be used.

List the program's performance benchmarks

Test your program with actual data.

Simulate a typical user's environment.

Under what conditions will your program work best? Similarly, under what conditions will it work poorly or not at all? Suggest alternatives.

Give the average running time with an average data set. Provide information (perhaps a graph) as to the overall performance of the program. Include in the reference manual at least one run showing in detail how the user should handle your program.

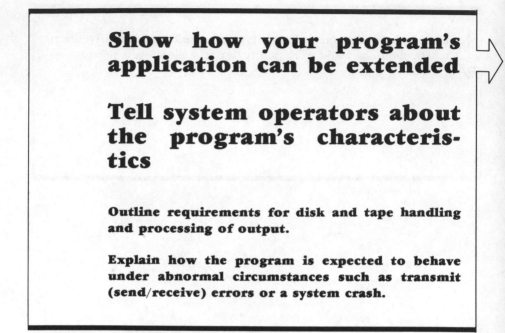

Show how your program's application can be extended

Tell system operators about the program's characteristics

Outline requirements for disk and tape handling and processing of output.

Explain how the program is expected to behave under abnormal circumstances such as transmit (send/receive) errors or a system crash.

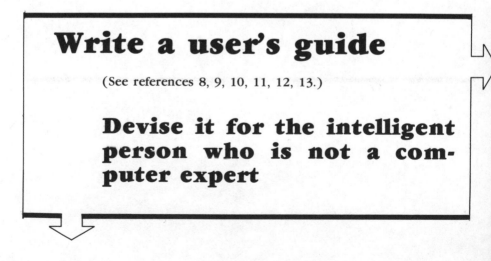

Write a user's guide

(See references 8, 9, 10, 11, 12, 13.)

Devise it for the intelligent person who is not a computer expert

Reproduce in the manual simulated displays of these applications; simulated system operator interactions; typical disk and tape procedures; and general steps that should be undertaken to prevent the loss, or to save as much as possible, of a run in an emergency.

Explain the following:

1 What is the purpose of the program?
2 What algorithm does it use? Give references to published literature on related problems.
3 What job control language is necessary to get the program to run?
4 What should the input look like, and how much of it can the program process at a time?

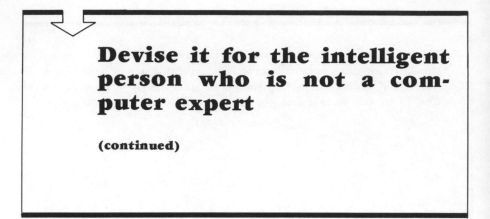

Devise it for the intelligent person who is not a computer expert

(continued)

Incorporate your knowledge of your program's users

Supply information on other programs that solve similar problems but may fit the user's needs better

5 What results should the user expect from the program?

6 What peripherals can be used with this program (plotter capabilities, graphics equipment, etc.)?

7 How can the user extend the capabilities of the program to solve more complex or slightly different problems?

Provide several sample runs as a guide to use of the program.

For whom is this program intended? An author of a book always must keep his or her reader in mind; so should the author of a computer program.

Rate other available programs that solve similar problems according to

1 differences from your program,
2 availability,
3 running time and efficiency of results.

Tell the user where to find these other programs.

REFERENCES

1. Knut Bulow, "Programming in Book Format," *Datamation*, vol. 20, no. 10, October 1974, pages 85–86.

2. D. R. Judd, "The Documentation of Computer Programs," in *Software Engineering* (Infotech State of the Art Report), Infotech International Ltd., Maidenhead, Berkshire, U. K., 1972, pages 411–424.

3. R. S. Scowens and B. A. Wichmann, "The Definition of Comments in Programming Languages," *Software—Practice and Experience,* vol. 4, no. 2, April–June 1974, pages 181–188.

4. P. J. Brown, "Programming and Documenting Software Projects," *Computing Surveys,* vol. 6, no. 4, December 1974, pages 213–220.

5. J. Katzenelson, "Documentation and the Management of a Software Project," *Software—Practice and Experience,* vol. 1, no. 2, April–June 1971, pages 147–157.

6. Gerhard Goos, "Documentation," in *Software Engineering—An Advanced Course,* edited by F. L. Bauer, Springer-Verlag, Berlin, 1973, pages 385–394.

7. Daniel M. Berry, "Structured Documentation," *SIGPLAN Notices*, vol. 10, no. 11, November 1975, pages 7–12.

8. J. R. Mashey and D. W. Smith, "Documentation Tools and Techniques," in *Proceedings of the 2nd International Conference on Software Engineering* (October 13–15, 1976, San Francisco), IEEE Press, New York, pages 177–181.

9. Max Gray and Keith R. London, *Documentation Standards*, Brandon/Systems Press, Princeton, N. J., 1969.

10. Dorothy A. Walsh, *A Guide to Software Documentation*, Inter-ACT Corporation and McGraw-Hill Book Co., New York, 1969.

11. William L. Harper, *Data Processing Documentation: Standards, Procedures and Applications*, Prentice-Hall, Englewood Cliffs, N. J., 1972.

12. Thomas R. Gildersleeve, *Organizing and Documenting Data Processing Information*, Hayden Book Company, Rochelle Park, N. J., 1977.

13. J. Van Duyn, *Documentation Manual*, Petrocelli/Charter, New York, 1972.

BIBLIOGRAPHY

Structured Programming and Related Topics

Aron, Joel D., *The Program Development Process: Part 1—The Individual Programmer,* Addison-Wesley Publishing Co., Reading, Mass., 1974.

Baker, F. T., "Structured Programming in a Production Programming Environment," *IEEE Transactions on Software Engineering,* vol. SE-1, no. 2, June 1975, pages 241–252.

Bauer, Friedrich L., "Software and Software Engineering," *SIAM Review,* vol. 15, no. 2, April 1973, pages 469–480.

Bauer, Friedrich L., "Software Engineering," in *Software Engineering—An Advanced Course,* edited by F. L. Bauer, Springer-Verlag, Berlin, 1973, pages 522–545.

Bauer, Friedrich L. (editor), *Software Engineering—An Advanced Course,* Springer-Verlag, Berlin, 1973.

Boehm, Barry W., "Software and Its Impact: A Quantitative Assessment," *Datamation,* vol. 19, no. 5, May 1973, pages 48–59.

Boehm, Barry W., Charles E. Holmes, Gene R. Katkus, James P. Romanos, Robert C. McHenry, and E. Kent Gordon, "Structured Programming: A Quantitative Assessment," *Computer,* vol. 8, no. 6, June 1975, pages 38–54.

Boehm, Barry W. (editor), *Characteristics of Software Quality,* Elsevier North Holland, New York, 1978.

Boehm, Barry W., *Software Engineering,* TRW Software Series Report, TRW-SS-76-08, TRW Defense and Space Systems Group, Redondo Beach, Calif., October 1976.

Bohl, Marilyn, *A Guide for Programmers,* Prentice-Hall, Englewood Cliffs, N.J., 1978.

Bohl, Marilyn, *Tools for Structured Design,* Science Research Associates, Palo Alto, Calif., 1978.

Brooks, Frederick P., Jr., *The Mythical Man-Month—Essays on Software Engineering,* Addison-Wesley Publishing Co., Reading, Mass., 1975.

Brown, Robert R., John R. Brown, and John W. Brackett, "Structured Programming: Problems, Approaches, and Techniques," *Computer,* vol. 8, no. 6, June 1975, pages 55 – 61.

Buxton, John N., Peter Naur, and Brian Randell, *Software Engineering—Concepts and Techniques* (Proceedings of the NATO Conferences), Petrocelli/Charter, New York, 1976.

Conway, Richard, and David Gries, *Primer on Structured Programming,* Winthrop Publishers, Cambridge, Mass., 1976.

Dahl, Ole-Johan, Edsger W. Dijkstra, and C. A. R. Hoare, *Structured Programming,* Academic Press, New York, 1972.

Dijkstra, Edsger W., *A Discipline of Programming,* Prentice-Hall, Englewood Cliffs, N.J., 1976.

Endres, A. B., "An Analysis of Errors and Their Causes in System Programs," *IEEE Transactions on Software Engineering,* vol. SE-1, no 2, June 1975, pages 140 – 149.

Freeman, Peter, *Software Systems Principles: A Survey,* Science Research Associates, Palo Alto, Calif., 1975.

Gane, Chris and Trish Sarson, *Structured Systems Analysis: Tools and Techniques,* Prentice-Hall, Englewood Cliffs, N.J., 1979.

Gilb, Tom, *Software Metrics,* Winthrop Publishers, Cambridge, Mass., 1977.

Gilb, Tom, and Gerald Weinberg, *Humanized Input,* Winthrop Publishers, Cambridge, Mass., 1977.

Glass, Robert L., *Software Reliability Guidebook,* Prentice-Hall, Englewood Cliffs, N.J., 1979.

Grosse, Eric, *Software Restyling in Graphics and Programming Languages,* Stanford University, Computer Science Department, Stanford, Calif., Technical Report No. STAN-CS-78-663, September 1978.

Hecht, Matthew S., *Flow Analysis of Computer Programs,* Elsevier North-Holland, New York, 1977.

Henderson, P., R. B. Gimson and M. M. Martin, *Modularisation of Large Programs,* University of Newcastle upon Tyne, Computing Laboratory, Newcastle upon Tyne, U.K., Technical Report No. 128, August 1978.

Hibbard, P. G., and S. A. Schuman (editors), *Constructing Quality Software* (Proceedings of the IFIP Working Conference on Constructing Quality Software, 1977), North-Holland Publishing Co., Amsterdam, 1978.

Higgins, David A., *Program Design and Construction,* Prentice-Hall, Englewood Cliffs, N.J., 1979.

Holt, Richard C., G. Scott Graham, Edward D. Lazowska, and Mark A. Scott, *Structured Concurrent Programming with Systems Applications,* Addison-Wesley Publishing Co., Reading, Mass., 1978.

Hughes, Joan K., and Jay I. Michtom, *A Structured Approach To Programming*, Prentice-Hall, Englewood Cliffs, N.J., 1977.

Infotech International Limited, *Software Testing: Vol. 1—Analysis and Bibliography*, Infotech International Ltd., Maidenhead, Berkshire, U.K., 1979.

Infotech International Limited, *Software Testing: Vol. 2—Invited Papers*, Infotech International Ltd., Maidenhead, Berkshire, U.K., 1979.

Jackson, Michael A., *Principles of Program Design*, Academic Press, New York, 1975.

Jensen, Randall W., and Charles C. Tonies, *Software Engineering*, Prentice-Hall, Englewood Cliffs, N.J., 1979.

Kernighan, Brian W., and P. J. Plauger, *The Elements of Programming Style* (2nd edition), McGraw-Hill Book Co., New York, 1978.

Kernighan, Brian W., and P. J. Plauger, "Programming Style: Examples and Counterexamples," *Computing Surveys,* vol. 6, no. 4, December 1974, pages 303 – 319.

Kernighan, Brian W., and P. J. Plauger, *Software Tools,* Addison-Wesley Publishing Co., Reading, Mass., 1976.

Knuth, Donald Ervin, *The Art of Computer Programming: Vol. 1 —Fundamental Algorithms* (2nd edition), Addison-Wesley Publishing Co., Reading, Mass., 1973.

Knuth, Donald Ervin, *The Art of Computer Programming: Vol. 2 —Seminumerical Algorithms,* Addison-Wesley Publishing Co., Reading, Mass., 1969.

Knuth, Donald Ervin, *The Art of Computer Programming: Vol. 3 —Sorting and Searching,* Addison-Wesley Publishing Co., Reading, Mass., 1973.

Knuth, Donald Ervin, "An Empirical Study of FORTRAN Programs," *Software—Practice and Experience,* vol. 1, no. 2, April – June 1971, pages 105 – 133.

Knuth, Donald Ervin, *TAU EPSILON CHI—A System for Technical Text,* Stanford University, Computer Science Department, Stanford, Caif., Technical Report No. STAN-CS-78-675, September 1978.

Ledgard, Henry F., *Programming Proverbs,* Hayden Book Co., Rochelle Park, N.J., 1975.

Mathis, Robert F., "Flow Trace of a Structured Program" *SIGPLAN Notices,* vol. 10, no. 4, April 1975, pages 33 – 37.

Maurer, W. D., "The Modification Index Method of Generating Verification Conditions," in *Proceedings of the 15th Annual ACM South-Eastern Regional Conference,* April 1977, pages 426 – 440.

McClure, Carma L., "Structured Programming in COBOL," *SIGPLAN Notices,* vol. 10, no. 4, April 1975, pages 25 – 33.

McGowan, Clement, "Structured Programming: A Review of Some Practical Concepts," *Computer,* vol. 8, no. 6, June 1975, pages 25 – 30.

McGowan, Clement L., and John R. Kelly, *Top-Down Structured Programming Techniques,* Petrocelli/Charter, New York, 1975.

Mills, Harlan D., *Mathematical Foundations for Structured Programming,* Report No. FSC 72-6012, IBM Federal Systems Division, Gaithersburg, Md., February 1972.

Mills, Harlan D., *Chief Programmer Teams: Principles and Procedures,* Report No. FSC 71-5108, IBM Federal Systems Division, Gaithersburg, Md., June 1972.

Mills, Harlan D., *How to Write Correct Programs and Know It,* Report No. FSC 73-5008, IBM Federal Systems Division, Gaithersburg, Md., February 1973.

Mills, Harlan D., "The New Math of Computer Programming," *Communications of the ACM,* vol. 18, no. 1, January 1975, pages 43–48.

Mills, Harlan D., "Software Development," *IEEE Transactions on Software Engineering,* vol. SE-2, no. 4, December 1976, pages 265–273.

Myers, Glenford J., *Reliable Software Through Composite Design,* Petrocelli/Charter, New York, 1975.

Myers, Glenford J., *Composite Structured Design,* Van Nostrand Reinhold, New York, 1978.

Myers, Glenford J., *Software Reliability—Principles and Practice,* John Wiley & Sons, New York, 1976.

Myers, Glenford J., *The Art of Software Testing,* John Wiley & Sons, New York, 1979.

Naur, Peter, *Concise Survey of Computer Methods,* Petrocelli/Charter, New York, 1974.

Noonan, Robert E., "Structured Programming and Formal Specification," *IEEE Transactions on Software Engineering,* vol. SE-1, no. 4, December 1975, pages 421–425.

Ogdin, Carol Anne, *Software Design for Microcomputers,* Prentice-Hall, Englewood Cliffs, N.J., 1978.

Parnas, D. L., "On the Criteria to Be Used in Decomposing Systems into Modules," *Communications of the ACM,* vol. 15, no. 12, December 1972, pages 1053–1058.

Ross, Douglas T., J. B. Goodenough, and C. A. Irvine, "Software Engineering: Process, Principles, and Goals," *Computer,* vol. 8, no. 5, May 1975, pages 17–27.

Ross, Douglas T., and John W. Brackett, "An Approach to Structured Analysis," *Computer Decisions,* vol. 8, no. 9, September 1976, pages 40–44.

Satterthwaite, Edwin H., Jr., *Source Language Debugging Tools,* Stanford University, Computer Science Department, Stanford, Calif., Ph. D. Thesis, Technical Report No. STAN-CS-75-494, May 1975.

Schaefer, Marvin, *A Mathematical Theory of Global Program Optimization,* Prentice-Hall, Englewood Cliffs, N.J., 1973.

Shneiderman, Ben, "Improving the Human Factors Aspect of Database Interactions," *ACM Transactions on Database Systems,* vol. 3, no. 4, December 1978, pages 417–439.

Shneiderman, Ben, *A Review of Design Techniques for Programs and Data,* Indiana University, Computer Science Dept., Bloomington, Ind., Technical Report No. 25, April 1975.

Simmons, Dick B., "The Art of Writing Large Programs," *Computer,* vol. 5, no. 2, March–April 1972, pages 43–49.

Stevens, Wayne P., Glenford J. Myers, and Larry L. Constantine, "Structured Design," *IBM Systems Journal,* vol. 13, no. 2, 1974, pages 115–139.

Swann, Gloria, *Top-Down Structured Design Techniques,* Petrocelli/Charter, New York, 1978.

Tausworthe, Robert C., *Standardized Development of Computer Software,* Prentice-Hall, Englewood Cliffs, N.J., 1977.

Turski, Wladislaw M., *Computer Programming Methodology,* Heyden & Son Ltd., London, 1978.

Van Tassel, Dennie, *Program Style, Design, Efficiency, Debugging, and Testing* (2nd edition), Prentice-Hall, Englewood Cliffs, N.J., 1978.

Warnier, Jean Dominique, *Logical Construction of Programs,* Van Nostrand Reinhold, New York, 1976.

Wasserman, Anthony I., Laszlo A. Belady, S. L. Gerhart, Edward F. Miller, Jr., William M. Waite, and William A. Wulf, "Software Engineering: The Turning Point," *Computer,* vol. 11, no. 9, September 1978, pages 30–41.

Weinberg, Gerald M., *The Psychology of Computer Programming,* Van Nostrand Reinhold, New York, 1971.

Weinberg, Gerald M., "The Psychology of Improved Programming Performance," *Datamation,* vol. 17, no. 11, November 1972, pages 82–85.

Weinberg, Gerald (editor), *Pragmatic programming and sensible software,* Online Conferences Ltd., Uxbridge, U.K., 1978.

Weinberg, Victor, *Structured Analysis,* Yourdon Press, New York, 1978.

Wilkes, Maurice V., "Software Engineering and Structured Programming," *IEEE Transactions on Software Engineering,* vol. SE-2, no. 4, December 1976, pages 274–276.

Wirth, Niklaus, *Systematic Programming: An Introduction,* Prentice-Hall, Englewood Cliffs, N.J., 1973.

Yeh, Raymond T., (editor), *Current Trends in Programming Methodology: Vol. 1—Software Specification and Design,* Prentice-Hall, Englewood Cliffs, N.J., 1977.

Yeh, Raymond T. (editor), *Current Trends in Programming Methodology: Vol. 2—Program Validation,* Prentice-Hall, Englewood Cliffs, N.J., 1977.

Yeh, Raymond T., and K. Mandi Chandy (editors), *Current Trends in Programming Methodology: Vol. 3—Software Modeling,* Prentice-Hall, Englewood Cliffs, N.J., 1978.

Yeh, Raymond T. (editor), *Current Trends in Programming Methodology: Vol. 4—Data Structuring,* Prentice-Hall, Englewood Cliffs, N.J., 1978.

Yohe, J. M., "An Overview of Programming Practices," *Computing Surveys,* vol. 6, no. 4, December 1974, pages 221–245.

Yourdon, Edward, *Techniques of Program Structure and Design,* Prentice-Hall, Englewood Cliffs, N.J., 1975.

Yourdon, Edward, and Larry L. Constantine, *Structured Design: Fundamentals of a Discipline of Computer Program and Systems Design,* Prentice-Hall, Englewood Cliffs, N.J., 1979.

Zelkowitz, Marvin V., "Perspectives on Software Engineering," *Computing Surveys,* vol. 10, no. 2, June 1978, pages 197–216.

Zelkowitz, Marvin V., Alan C. Shaw, and John D. Gannon, *Principles of Software Engineering and Design,* Prentice-Hall, Englewood Cliffs, N.J., 1979.

Programming Languages

ALGOL

Ekman, Torgil, and Carl-Erik Fröberg, *Introduction to ALGOL Programming* (3rd edition), Studentlitteratur/Oxford University Press, London, 1971.

Kieburtz, Richard B., *Structured Programming and Problem Solving with ALGOL W,* Prentice-Hall, Englewood Cliffs, N.J., 1975.

Lindsey, Charles H., and Sietse G. van der Meulen, *Informal Introduction to ALGOL 68,* North-Holland Publishing Co., Amsterdam, 1971.

APL

Geller, Dennis P., and Daniel P. Freedman, *Structured Programming in APL,* Winthrop Publishers, Cambridge, Mass., 1976.

Iverson, Kenneth E., *A Programming Language,* John Wiley & Sons, New York, 1962.

Polivka, Raymond, and S. Pakin, *APL: The Language and Its Usage,* Prentice-Hall, Englewood Cliffs, N.J., 1975.

BASIC

Kemeny, John G., and Thomas E. Kurtz, *BASIC Programming* (2nd edition), John Wiley & Sons, New York, 1971.

Ledin, George, Jr., *A Structured Approach to General BASIC,* Boyd & Fraser Publishing Co., San Francisco, 1978.

Marateck, Samuel A., *BASIC,* Academic Press, New York, 1975.

COBOL

Feingold, Carl, *Fundamentals of Structured COBOL* (3rd edition), Wm. C. Brown Co., Dubuque, Iowa, 1978.

Grauer, Robert T., and Marshal A. Crawford, *COBOL—A Pragmatic Approach,* Prentice-Hall, Englewood Cliffs, N.J., 1978.

McCracken, Daniel D., and Umberto Garbassi, *A Guide to COBOL Programming* (2nd edition), John Wiley & Sons, New York, 1970.

Murach, Mike, *Standard COBOL* (2nd edition), Science Research Associates, Palo Alto, Calif., 1975.

FORTRAN

Didday, Richard L., and Rex L. Page, *FORTRAN for Humans* (2nd edition), West Publishing Co., St. Paul, Minn., 1977.

Friedman, Frank L., and Elliot B. Koffman, *Problem Solving and Structured Programming in FORTRAN,* Addison-Wesley Publishing Co., Reading, Mass., 1977.

Kreitzberg, Charles B., and Ben Shneiderman, *FORTRAN Programming—A Spiral Approach,* Harcourt Brace Jovanovich, New York, 1975.

McCracken, Daniel Delbert, *A Guide to FORTRAN IV Programming* (2nd edition), John Wiley & Sons, New York, 1972.

GPSS

Greenberg, Stanley, *GPSS Primer,* John Wiley & Sons, New York, 1972.

LISP

Friedman, Daniel P., *The Little LISPer,* Science Research Associates, Palo Alto, Calif., 1974.

McCarthy, John, Paul W. Abrahams, Daniel J. Edwards, Timothy P. Hart, and Michael I. Levin, *LISP 1.5 Programmer's Manual* (2nd edition), MIT Press, Cambridge, Mass., 1965.

Siklossy, Laurent, *Let's Talk LISP,* Prentice-Hall, Englewood Cliffs, N.J., 1976.

Weissman, Clark, *LISP 1.5 Primer,* Dickenson Publishing Co., Belmont, Calif., 1967.

PASCAL

Findlay, William, and David A. Watt, *PASCAL—An Introduction to Methodical Programming,* Computer Science Press, Potomac, Md., 1978.

Grogono, Peter, *Programming in PASCAL,* Addison-Wesley Publishing Co., Reading, Mass., 1978.

Jensen, Kathleen, and Niklaus Wirth, *PASCAL User Manual and Report* (2nd edition), Springer-Verlag, Berlin, 1975.

Schneider, G. Michael, Steven W. Weingart, and David M. Perlman, *An Introduction to Programming and Problem Solving with PASCAL,* John Wiley & Sons, New York, 1978.

PL/1

Bates, Frank, and Mary L. Douglas, *Programming Language/One— With Structured Programming* (3rd edition), Prentice-Hall, Englewood Cliffs, N.J., 1975.

Conway, Richard, *A Primer on Disciplined Programming Using PL/1, PL/CS and PL/CT,* Winthrop Publishers, Cambridge, Mass., 1978.

Pollack, Seymour V., and Theodore D. Sterling, *A Guide to PL/1* (2nd edition), Holt, Rinehart and Winston, New York, 1976.

Ruston, Henry, *Programming with PL/1,* McGraw-Hill Book Co., New York, 1978.

RPG

Little, Joyce Currie, *RPG: Report Program Generator,* Prentice-Hall, Englewood Cliffs, N.J., 1971.

SIMULA

Birtwistle, Graham M., Ole-Johan Dahl, Bjørn Myhrhaug, and Kristen Nygaard, *SIMULA BEGIN,* Petrocelli/Charter, New York, 1973.

SNOBOL

Forte, Allen, *SNOBOL3 Primer: An Introduction to the Computer Programming Language,* MIT Press, Cambridge, Mass., 1967.

Griswold, Ralph E., J. F. Poage, and I. P. Polonsky, *The SNOBOL 4 Programming Language,* (2nd edition), Prentice-Hall, Englewood Cliffs, N.J., 1971.

Griswold, Ralph E., and Madge T. Griswold, *A SNOBOL4 Primer,* Prentice-Hall, Englewood Cliffs, N.J., 1973.

Newsted, Peter R., *SNOBOL: An Introduction to Programming,* Hayden Book Co., Rochelle Park, N.J., 1975.

Flowcharting and Decision Tables

Bohl, Marilyn, *Flowcharting Techniques,* Science Research Associates, Palo Alto, Calif., 1971.

Chapin, Ned, *Flowcharts,* Petrocelli/Charter, New York, 1971.

Elliott, Ronald E., *Problem Solving and Flowcharting,* Reston Publishers, Reston, Va., 1972.

Farina, Mario V., *Flowcharting,* Prentice-Hall, Englewood Cliffs, N.J., 1970.

Gleim, George A., *Program Flowcharting,* Holt, Rinehart and Winston, New York, 1970.

Lehner, John K., *Flowcharting: An Introductory Text and Workbook,* Auerbach Publishers, New York, 1972.

Lindsey, C. H., "Structure Charts—A Structured Alternative to Flowcharts," *SIGPLAN Notices,* vol. 12, no. 11, November 1977, pages 36–49.

London, Keith R., *Decision Tables,* Petrocelli/Charter, New York, 1972.

McDaniel, Herman, *Decision Table Software—A Handbook,* Brandon/Systems Press, Princeton, N.J., 1970.

McInerney, Thomas F., and Andre J. Valee, *A Student's Guide to Flowcharting,* Prentice-Hall, Englewood Cliffs, N.J., 1973.

McQuigg, James D., and Alta M. Harness, *Flowcharting,* Houghton-Mifflin, Boston, 1970.

Montalbano, Michael S., "Tables, Flowcharts and Program Logic," *IBM Systems Journal,* vol. 1, no. 1, September 1962, pages 51 – 63.

Montalbano, Michael S., *Decision Tables,* Science Research Associates, Palo Alto, Calif., 1974.

Myers, H. J., "Compiling Optimized Code from Decision Tables," *IBM Journal of Research and Development,* vol. 16, no. 5, September 1972, pages 489 – 503.

Nassi, I., and Ben Shneiderman, "Flowchart Techniques for Structured Programming," *SIGPLAN Notices,* vol. 8, no. 8, August 1973, pages 12 – 26.

Pollack, Solomon R., Harry T. Hicks Jr., and William J. Harrison, *Decision Tables: Theory and Practice,* John Wiley & Sons, New York, 1971.

Pooch, Udo W., "Translation of Decision Tables," *Computing Surveys,* vol. 6, no. 2, June 1974, pages 125 – 151.

Schriber, Thomas J., *Fundamentals of Flowcharting,* John Wiley & Sons, New York, 1969.

Shelly, Gary B., and Thomas J. Cashman, *Introduction to Flowcharting and Computer Programming Logic,* Anaheim Publishing Co., Fullerton, Calif., 1972.

Wayne, Mark, *Flowcharting Concepts and Data Processing Techniques: A Self-Instructional Guide,* Canfield Press, San Francisco, 1973.

Performance Evaluation

Benwell, Nicholas, *Benchmarking—Computer Evaluation and Measurement,* Halstead Press, New York, 1975.

Ferrari, Domenico, *Computer Systems Performance Evaluation,* Prentice-Hall, Englewood Cliffs, N.J., 1978.

Freiberger, Walter (Ed.), *Statistical Computer Performance Evaluation,* Academic Press, New York, 1972.

Hellerman, Herbert, and Thomas F. Conroy, *Computer System Performance,* McGraw-Hill Book Co., New York, 1975.

Infotech International Limited, *Performance Modelling and Prediction: Vol. 1—Analysis and Bibliography,* Infotech International Ltd., Maidenhead, Berkshire, U.K., 1977.

Infotech International Limited, *Performance Modelling and Prediction: Vol. 2—Invited Papers,* Infotech International Ltd., Maidenhead, Berkshire, U.K., 1977.

Svobodova, Liba, *Computer Performance Measurement and Evaluation Methods—Analysis and Applications,* Elsevier North Holland, New York, 1976.

AUTHOR INDEX

SUBJECT INDEX